DEMCO

SUSAN BOYLE

DREAMS CAN COME TRUE

ALICE MONTGOMERY

THORNDIKE
WINDSOR
PARAGON

This Large Print edition is published by Thorndike Press, Waterville, Maine, USA and by BBC Audiobooks Ltd, Bath, England.
Thorndike Press, a part of Gale, Cengage Learning.
Copyright © 2010 by Alice Montgomery.
The moral right of the author has been asserted.

ALL RIGHTS RESERVED
Thorndike Press® Large Print Biography.
The text of this Large Print edition is unabridged.
Other aspects of the book may vary from the original edition.
Set in 16 pt. Plantin.

LIBRARY OF CONGRESS CATALOGING-IN-PUBLICATION DATA

Montgomery, Alice.
   Susan Boyle : dreams can come true / by Alice Montgomery.
  — Large print ed.
    p. cm.
   ISBN-13: 978-1-4104-2680-2 (hardcover)
   ISBN-10: 1-4104-2680-7 (hardcover)
   1. Boyle, Susan, 1961– 2. Singers—Scotland—Biography.
 I. Title.
 ML420.B763M66 2010
 782.42164092—dc22
 [B]
                                      2010005955

BRITISH LIBRARY CATALOGUING-IN-PUBLICATION DATA AVAILABLE

Published in 2010 in the U.S. by arrangement with The Overlook Press, Peter Mayer Publishers, Inc.
Published in 2010 in the U.K. by arrangement with Penguin Books Ltd.

U.K. Hardcover: 978 1 408 48667 2 (Windsor Large Print)
U.K. Softcover: 978 1 408 48668 9 (Paragon Large Print)

Printed in the United States of America
1 2 3 4 5 6 7 14 13 12 11 10

CONTENTS

LIST OF ILLUSTRATIONS

Susan's beloved mother, Bridget, posing with Mary Boyle and Bridie Boyle.
Photonews Scotland/Rex Features

Susan's father, Patrick Boyle, during his service in the Royal Engineers during the Second World War.
Photonews Scotland/Rex Features

Susan and her family: Gerard, James, John, Kathleen, Joe, Bridie, Mary, Susan, Patrick (father) and Bridget (mother).
Photonews Scotland/Rex Features

Susan's home in Blackburn, near Broxburn, West Lothian.
Tina Norris/Rex Features

Fred O'Neil, who gave Susan singing lessons for several years and nurtured her incredible talent.

7

Tina Norris/Rex Features

Singing has always been Susan's passion!
PA Photos

Shots of Susan at home taken during the *Britain's Got Talent* series.
Tina Norris/Rex Features

The formidable *Britain's Got Talent* judges. Piers Morgan, Amanda Holden and Simon Cowell.
Ken McKay/Rex Features

A woman viewing the incredible YouTube video clip of Susan's first performance of 'I Dreamed a Dream' on *Britain's Got Talent.*
Jonathan Hordle/Rex Features

In the run-up to the final, bookmakers were in a flurry of activity as the public placed bets on the final few contestants. Susan was the firm favourite at Ladbroke's bookmakers in her hometown.
Getty Images

As the series reached its finale, it was clear that the most serious threat to Susan's victory was the brilliantly gymnastic dance troupe, Diversity.

Ken McKay/Rex Features

However, if Ant and Dec, the show's jovial hosts, had the inside scoop on which way the audience was going to vote in the final, they certainly weren't letting on.
David Fisher/Rex Features

Supporters wearing Susan masks gather in her hometown to watch the final of *Britain's Got Talent*.
Getty Images

Susan greets young fans at the door of her house.
Photonews Scotland/Rex Features

Susan poses with two fans, Mathew Balderston and Kevin Hepworth, who drove for three hours from Alloa in order to meet their hero.
Mirrorpix

Susan wows fans during the opening show of the *Britain's Got Talent* live tour at the National Indoor Arena in Birmingham, in front of a packed audience of 5,000.
Ken McKay/Rex Features

Susan smiles for the cameras with her doc-

tor, Sarah Latzof, after her brief stay at The Priory.
Rex Features

Susan getting ready to board a plane from Heathrow Airport . . .
Dennis Stone/Rex Features

. . . and arriving at Los Angeles International Airport on her first trip to America.
Rex Features

Susan's beloved cat, Pebbles, became a celebrity in her own right — here, she's shielded from the snapping lights of photographers!
Alistair Linford/Rex Features

Susan performing as a guest on *America's Got Talent.* In her US TV singing debut, she covered the Rolling Stones track 'Wild Horses', as well as singing 'I Dreamed a Dream', the song that originally catapulted her to fame in the UK.
NBCUPHOTOBANK/Rex Features

As part of its *People of the Year* show, NBC took a look at the most fascinating, inspirational and heroic figures of 2009. Susan was invited to appear as a guest and was inter-

viewed by Matt Lauer.
NBCUPHOTOBANK/Rex Features

Susan is greeted by throngs of fans when she arrives at JFK Airport, New York.
Henry Lamb/Photowire/BEI/Rex Features

More fans gather to watch Susan perform at *The Today Show* in New York.
Debra L. Rothenberg/Rex Features; NBCUPHOTOBANK/Rex Features

Susan takes to the stage at *The Today Show,* revels in the limelight and delights the audience.
Greg Allen/Rex Features; Erik Pendzich/ Rex/Rex Features; NBCUPHOTOBANK/ Rex Features

Back home in Blackburn after her incredible US trip, Susan poses in her dressing gown for the photographers gathered outside her house, hoping to catch a glimpse of her new, post-makeover look.
Daniel Gilfeather/Rex Features

Susan was to capture the hearts of not just Britain and America, but the whole world! She has appeared on major chat shows throughout Europe. Here she poses with

11

French television presenter Michel Drucker.
Sipa Press/Rex Features

As part of her trip to Europe, Susan performs on German television show *Menschen 2009*.
PA Photos

German television presenter Thomas Gottschalk presents a bouquet of flowers to Susan after her performance on the show.
PA Photos

Susan returns to her home in Blackburn. She may have triumphantly conquered the world, but home is still very much where her heart is.
PA Photos

Every effort has been made to trace copyright holders. The publishers will be glad to rectify in future editions any errors or omissions brought to their attention.

PROLOGUE: NEW YORK, NOVEMBER 2009

The Big Apple had never seen anything like it. Susan Boyle, the mild mannered Scottish spinster who had sprung from complete obscurity only seven months previously, held the crowd in thrall. Dressed in an elegant black coat, and wearing a red knitted scarf, a look that was becoming her trademark, she stood in front of a huge crowd at the Rockefeller Center, where she was performing live on NBC's *Today* show. Many in the crowd, who were giving her the kind of welcome more commonly reserved for superstars, were also wearing red scarves: it was a way of showing support and solidarity. It was a way of showing SuBo, as she was now affectionately known, that they were true fans.

Although she still didn't entirely fit the image many people had of a performer who was set to sell in the millions, Susan looked like a different woman from the one who had staggered viewers of *Britain's Got Talent* just a short while earlier. Her hair, previously wild and frizzy, had been trimmed into an elegant brunette bob; her eyebrows had been tamed; her face carefully made up and scarlet nail varnish glittered on her fingernails. She was transformed by the power of her growing stardom, her talent and the deep reserve of affection the public felt for her.

This, a thirty-minute live set for *Today,* was the culmination of a month-long publicity drive to herald the release of Susan's first album, and although it was the kind of occasion that would have tested the nerves of many a seasoned performer, she carried it off with aplomb. *Today* show hosts Matt Lauer and Meredith Vieira chatted to Susan in front of the cheering crowd: it was a 'great achievement', she acknowledged, to have come from a small town in Scotland to where she was now — and all in such a short space of time. 'It feels very surreal, as if it's not really happening,' she went on. 'I've grown up a bit and become more of a lady. I don't swing my hips as much.'

Susan's replies to her hosts' questions weren't lengthy — when she spoke she still had a little shyness about her — but there was no awkwardness either, especially given that she was standing in front of a crowd brandishing placards bearing her name and various slogans associated with her — 'I dreamed a dream too' being a typical example. All things considered, Susan seemed remarkably calm, composed even. Then the moment everyone had been waiting for happened. As Susan stepped in front of the microphone, she was almost glowing; she opened her mouth and burst into song. Her remarkable voice soared above the crowd and into the New York sky as she sang 'I Dreamed A Dream', followed by the Rolling Stones' 'Wild Horses' and rounded off by 'Cry Me A River'. The crowd was stunned and burst into wild applause.

All the songs were familiar: 'I Dreamed A Dream' was the number with which she'd débuted in the national consciousness, while 'Wild Horses' was to be her album's first single. There was some joshing about the fact that Susan Boyle and the Rolling Stones were an unlikely coupling, but she carried it off. One critic, the *Mirror*'s Paul McNamee, pointed out that while the Stones sang it as a song about a fading relationship, Susan imbued it with a quality of hope, albeit tinged with tragedy, 'elements of a life lived on the edge of society, the outsider mocked by all.'

All the songs were from her new album, *I Dreamed A Dream,* which Susan had dedicated to her mother and which was making musical history. It had already become the biggest pre-ordered album since the online store Amazon started selling discs, and when it was released, 701,000 copies sold in the first week. SuBo was breaking records everywhere she turned: the CD went on to become the highest-selling ever for a female artist's début album since Nielsen Sound-Scan started tracking sales back in 1991, while back in the UK, the album sold 410,000 copies and was about to become the bestselling début album ever, going straight in at number one. To put this in context, Susan had managed to sell more advance copies of her CD than U2, Bruce Springsteen or Coldplay, some of the biggest names in the business. She was, quite simply, a phenomenon. There had never been anything like this before. Although reality television had produced its fair share of stars who had gone on to map out enduring careers, they were all young and all, including the boys, pretty. Susan, however, was not only knocking them all into a cocked hat, she was doing the same to established stars who appeared to have

16

more mainstream appeal than her. It would seem that the little woman with the big voice had touched a raw nerve in audiences nationwide. SuBo had arrived and SuBo was a star.

Simon Cowell, who essentially discovered Susan on *Britain's Got Talent,* and who had become her protector and mentor, was delighted, as well he might have been. 'She did it her way and made a dream come true,' he told *Sky News.* 'I'm incredibly proud of her. The success could not have happened to a lovelier person. In *Britain's Got Talent,* she opened her mouth and the world fell in love with her, which is why her album has been the fastest selling of any woman making her début. She's amazing.'

Piers Morgan, another of the judges on *Britain's Got Talent,* was equally proud of the show's protégé. 'I was probably one of the few people in Britain who did expect this,' he told *Sky.* 'I could tell from America in particular that she was a phenomenon. Something we've not seen from any talent show in the history of talent shows. The ultimate underdog, she had this amazing talent, which was never recognized, and then she took her moment. Quite an amazing story.'

It certainly was, and given the high expectations that had been placed on her shoulders, she was coping incredibly well, too. Sales were, in fact, exceeding the already high hopes of the record company. The power of Susan's influence, whether she realized it or not, was so great it touched even the mighty Rolling Stones. In the wake of Susan's success with their old song, they re-released 'Wild Horses' themselves. It seemed that everything Susan touched was turning to gold — quite an achievement for a lady with learning disabilities from an extremely sheltered background. As she rather bashfully admitted, this was her first time in New York, and while most of it was to be spent working, she hoped for a little time to look around. This wasn't, however, her first trip to the States. From being a resolute homebody, Susan was turning into an international traveller, and her feet had barely touched the ground during the previous few months.

Her fans at the Rockefeller Center that day couldn't get enough of her. Chanting her name, cheering her on and calling out for more, they adored her, not least because, although she was Scottish and had come to prominence on a British TV show, Susan was the American dream come true. There, in the land of the free, they believed that anyone could make something of themselves if they tried hard enough, and no one was making more of herself or trying harder than Susan Boyle. Even her unworldliness was appealing: Susan was no glamour puss, dolled up to the nines to disguise an almost total absence of talent; instead her talent, in its rawest form, was fighting its way out. Susan was both modest and extraordinary. It was a take on the Cinderella story that had rarely been seen before.

The very speed with which it was all happening, however, was beginning to bring its own problems. It was no secret that Susan was fragile, and in the aftermath of *Britain's Got Talent,* she spent a short time in The Priory clinic, suffering from stress and, most likely, as an emotional reaction to her extraordinary fate. Now it seemed there was a danger it was happening again.

In the wake of her appearance on the *Today* show, Susan was taken to the nearby Rock Center Café to meet some of her fans. They had a present for her, and it was quite some present: a patchwork quilt, that had been put together by an international network of admirers from twenty-eight countries, including the UK, the States, Australia, Canada, Mexico, Poland, Japan and

Antarctica.

For a woman who had endured bullying, both as a child and an adult, this was the ultimate vindication: she was loved everywhere, by everyone, all over the world. Surely, this was proof, if proof were needed, that Susan's problems were behind her and that she was about to start a new phase in her life?

A new life might have been beginning, but Susan's problems had not, alas, disappeared. Right from the word go there had been concerns that someone as fragile as Susan might find it hard to deal with all the attention her fame brought, and according to some people, this had already turned out to be the case. Rather than chatting to her new fans, Susan became increasingly withdrawn, gazing into the distance and sucking her thumb. An aide, clearly realizing that something was wrong, came to her side, but Susan, looking visibly distressed, waved her away. Moments later, she put her head in her hands and wept.

One issue was clearly exhaustion: the New York trip marked the culmination of a whirlwind tour of the States, and she had just recorded an album. As much as anything, the poor woman was in need of a rest. To her credit, she snapped out of it pretty quickly: as soon as she realized she was being watched, Susan put on a more cheerful expression and did a little dance. But her brave face couldn't allay fears that it was all too much, too soon.

On the other hand, some observers were adamant that the pictures were not what they seemed. Susan had put her thumb in her mouth as a joke, they said, to illustrate to onlookers that she didn't want to behave like a baby. And for someone new to the public eye, and having to learn the tricks of the trade exceedingly fast, she simply hadn't realized how bad the pictures would look. Certainly Susan, like almost all modern-day celebrities, was beginning to realize she couldn't switch the attention off: she was either in the public eye or she wasn't. And just for the moment, at least, she seemed destined to stay there.

Doubts about her fragility were not quelled fast. The people surrounding Susan, most notably the *Britain's Got Talent* team, had become rather touchy on the subject of Susan's mental state and whether they were right to expose Susan to the glare of the limelight and the international stage. If truth be told, their feelings were understandable: they had, after all, taken Susan from humble circumstances and turned her, to her visible delight, into an international star.

But that, they said, was the point: she didn't want to go back to being the Susan Boyle of her pre−talent show days, and if she didn't want to, why should they? Even so, everyone concerned realized that the thumb-sucking incident had the potential to drum up a great deal of eyebrow raising, so a damage-limitation team snapped into action. 'She was just overjoyed and extremely touched with the reception she has had from everyone in America,' said her spokesman, adding that she had not broken down and that legal action would be taken against anyone who said she had.

Piers Morgan was equally irritated by suggestions that all might not be well. 'Susan, like all performers, has up and down moments,' he told *Sky News*. 'It's very pressurized performing in front of thousands of people, whoever you are. Barbra Streisand still gets nervous. John Lennon apparently was very nervous before every Beatles show. It's not a new phenomenon to Susan. I think she deals with the pressure very well now. She has very good people around her. Whenever I've seen her or spoken to her she's been remarkably relaxed, thoroughly enjoying it, and for everyone who still persists in saying, "She's cracking up, boiling over, she can't deal with it," well look at her. She's made one of the best albums of the year, she'll be the biggest-selling artist of all time, she's taking America by storm, she's loving every second, she looks amazing — I think the people that criticize her should shut up and enjoy the moment of Susan Boyle becoming the fastest-selling artist in history.'

She certainly rallied quickly. Such was the interest in her in the United States that plans were announced to make a television programme about her life, *I Dreamed A Dream: The Susan Boyle Story,* to be shown on both sides of the Atlantic. Meanwhile, Susan herself had tackled the issue of whether or not she would be able to cope with it all head on. 'There was a lot of attention,' she told Matt Lauer. 'I asked myself, "How do you cope with all this?" I did have a period of self-doubt where I felt I wasn't good enough. And there are times when, because I'm shy, I wished it would all go away. Sometimes you do think that, it's only human nature.'

There were other issues to consider as well, mainly brought about because Susan's experience was so unique. Unlike other singers who had become extremely famous,

Susan hadn't had much time to adapt to her new status, which made coping even more difficult. Hers had not been the traditional route up through clubs and smaller establishments, which is how most professional singers learn their trade — a hard slog that makes them well aware of their own worth. At times Susan herself must have felt that she hadn't paid her dues — for all that she had led a sheltered life, she hadn't experienced the years of endeavour and rejection that most singers have to endure. It would be surprising if she hadn't sometimes wondered whether she was worth all the fuss.

About one thing, though, Susan was adamant: she was very happy with her lot. 'I accept now that my life will never be the same,' she continued. 'And I don't want it to end. It's OK. It's just comfortable in my shoulders right now. I don't feel pressure just now. I just feel a sense of humility.'

The interview on the *Today* show was a revealing one, for Susan also tackled the other issue — the one that lay behind everything — head on. Until then, although there had been a good deal in the press about her mental ability, Susan hadn't really commented on the subject at length herself, although she had made passing reference to her condition, which was caused when she was starved of oxygen at birth. She was clearly going to have to talk about it at some point, however, as it increasingly became the elephant in the room. She finally spoke about it to Matt Lauer, pointing out that in many ways her new-found fame was exactly what she needed to help her to cope.

'I do have a slight disability — I had difficulty trying to express myself properly and music is a release for me,' she explained. If that didn't silence the doubters, nothing would, for in essence Susan was saying that what she couldn't put into words, she could put into song. This was her way of communicating with the rest of the world.

The teariness aside, Susan's trip to the United States had been a massive success, and one that had also allowed her to take stock. As she flew home, the sound of cheering and applause still ringing in her ears, there were decisions to be made, such as how to forge ahead? In the immediate wake of her stardom, Susan had been planning to move down to London full time, but those plans were now shelved. What she needed, as she and everyone around her realized, was complete security when she wasn't in front of a crowd, and that was best found at home.

Consequently, a more modest plan was hatched: Susan would buy the four-bedroom council house in Blackburn, West Lothian, where she had lived all of her life, not least because she didn't want to disrupt the existence of Pebbles, her much-loved cat. She was certainly able to afford her old home now. Estimates of her initial earnings varied wildly, with figures stretching from £100,000 to £6 million, but whatever the truth, one thing was certain: Susan's financial situation was about to be transformed. And when she returned to Scotland she was greeted, as expected, as a returning conquering hero.

Another concern, which swiftly proved to be unfounded, was that Susan would let it go to her head. In actual fact she seemed remarkably unfazed by her change of fortune. On returning to Scotland, where she had been advised to get some rest, Susan was photographed waving cheerily, clad in a polka-dot dressing gown and pyjamas, looking totally unselfconscious about being photographed in her nightwear. It brought to mind a very different woman who had also been surprised by photographers while wearing just a long T-shirt, but who had reacted very differently: Cherie Blair, the day after her husband was elected Prime Minister in May 1997. Whereas Cherie appeared flustered and uncomfortable about being photographed in such a revealing and unflattering light, it didn't appear to bother Susan. It seemed she was adapting to her new life quite well.

Even so, there were mixed reports from Susan's neighbours, who suddenly found they had a superstar in their midst. One, Teresa Miller, told the *Mirror* that Susan had 'definitely changed', although she was aware that there was nothing malevolent about it. Susan's situation was almost unprecedented, and she was learning to cope day-by-day. 'I said hello to her in the street the other day and she blanked me,' Teresa went on. 'Then on other days she's perfectly charming. It must be the stress getting to her. But I'll always be here for her if she needs me.'

Then there was Susan's new album, which she had apparently taken to playing at full blast. 'It was so loud on Thursday I couldn't hear Jeremy Kyle on TV!' said Teresa. 'It started about a week before it was released, so by the time it was on sale we already knew every track by heart. I think her favourite song is "Wild Horses" as that's the one she plays the most. We've also seen two ambulances and a doctor come to her house. Susan had told me she had been feeling pains in her stomach.'

On the whole, however, Susan's neighbours were very protective of her. She was one of their own; she had grown up in the community, and while she might have experienced difficulties with a few, isolated individuals, on the whole people just wanted to make sure she was all right. They knew about Susan's learning difficulties first hand and had seen her transformed in front of the whole world. They understood that she was subject to the kind of pressures that more robust individuals have difficulty dealing with, and they wanted to make sure she was able to cope.

Helen Barkhouse, who had looked after Susan's mother Bridget until she died in 2007, was another neighbour who portrayed Susan as sensitive, generous and not at all spoiled by fame. 'Susan was here wearing a black beret and a necklace and I told her how pretty she looked,' she told the *Mirror*. 'She took them off and gave them to me. After her mother's death Susan got really low. She once came up to me in the supermarket and said, "I really need a hug, can you give me a hug?" She might be a star, but whenever Susan comes home we'll make sure she's properly taken care of.'

It was certainly what Susan needed, because by now her album had débuted at number one in the charts, guaranteeing her even more attention. In her first audition for *Britain's Got Talent,* Susan had said she wanted to be as big as Elaine Paige. At the time, given her then unrefined appearance and having not yet proven the power of her voice, the viewer could have been forgiven for being a little doubtful. Now it was beginning to look as if this might actually be the case. 'It's fantastic,' was all a clearly overwhelmed Susan could say, but it was a lot more than that. It was an extraordinary achievement from a woman no one would ever have dreamed could become a star.

Simon Cowell, the ringmaster of this particular circus, bobbed up again. 'I'm incredibly proud of Susan and delighted for her,' he said. 'This success couldn't have happened to a more deserving person. Susan Boyle quite simply has broken the rules, her story is like a Hollywood movie, but this time it's real life and a really talented, nice lady who has won.'

It was the culmination of an extraordinary month, even by Susan's standards, and a mark of just how far she'd come. Elaine Paige wasn't the half of it: Susan had her sights set on even greater matters. Just a few weeks earlier, Susan, a devout Catholic, had expressed a wish to sing for Pope Benedict XVI: 'Apart from being a singer and being accepted by people and bringing them happiness, my biggest dream is to meet His Holiness the Pope,' she'd explained. 'I would love to sing "Panis Angelicus" for him. Religion is the backbone of my life; it has given me strength to go forward, in particular when my mother died.' It was an ambition that would have seemed unlikely a few months earlier, but now anything was possible. She'd already met one of her idols, Donny Osmond — 'It was a dream come true. He was lovely' — at his mansion in LA; was there anything Susan would not be able to do?

In the run-up to her trip to New York, two other people who were staggered by what was going on were Ant and Dec. The Geordie duo were the presenters of *Britain's Got Talent,* and while they weren't as closely linked with Susan as Simon Cowell, they were seasoned players in the entertainment world and had been utterly shocked by the media frenzy SuBo had whipped up. Far from having a non-stop route to the top, Ant and Dec had suffered plenty of setbacks along the way, so they knew from experience how tough the showbiz world can be.

They had hosted *Britain's Got Talent* from the outset, and if anyone had their finger on the audience's pulse, both within the studio and in the country at large, it was those two, and they professed themselves to be amazed.

'I have to say, even watching her performance then, the audience were great. The judges were kind of surprised,' said Ant. 'We thought, That's a nice story. I never anticipated it being as big as it would be. Never in a million years. She was really nice and a bit nervous and we didn't expect anything much of her. Then she brought the house down.'

Dec agreed. 'We talk about people being overnight sensations, but she literally was,' he said. 'She was the first global overnight superstar. To go from being that little lady in a small village in Scotland to being known all over the world and having famous Hollywood stars Twittering about you must have made her head spin.'

But Susan appeared to be coping, even though she could hardly believe what was going on. Her trip to New York wasn't her first visit to the States in this strange new life she was leading; she had already been to the centre of Planet Showbiz — Los Angeles — when she was working on her CD.

'There were great crowds waiting for us at

LA airport,' she told the *Daily Express*. 'It was quite something. Nothing a woman like me was used to. But I found Americans to be incredibly warm and friendly and very open. It was quite something to be in Hollywood. It's like stepping back in time, to another time and place. The hotel I was staying in? Apparently Frank Sinatra used to take his women back there. And I dipped my toes into the pool Grace Kelly swam in. I can't wait to visit again.'

There was also Susan's changed appearance, about which her delight was palpable. In her late forties, she suddenly looked more soignée than she ever had in her life. 'I brush up quite well,' she continued, giggling slightly, Cinderella wearing the glass slipper at last. 'I'm forty-eight . . . but it's only a number, for goodness' sake. It's a bit like a cygnet to a swan. Now I seem a sophisticated lady. But even though the outwardness has changed, inside I'm still the same, but a bit more refined in some ways. I keep reading that I've had Botox, and my teeth whitening but I haven't. I've just been working hard and lost a bit of weight.'

With the release of Susan's début album imminent, the publicity machine moved up a gear, and two very high-profile appearances were planned for her. The second was the aforementioned gig at the Rockefeller Center, but before that there would be a major appearance in the UK on Simon Cowell's other brain-child, *The X Factor,* and many people felt that for Susan this was the biggest triumph of all.

It was said that she thought her only chance of fame came from an appearance on *Britain's Got Talent,* and not its counterpart, because *The X Factor* is more looks oriented. Susan felt that because of this she would never have got through the auditions. Now she was being asked to appear on *X Factor* not as a contestant, but as a performer, the latest in a line of extremely high-profile singers that included *X Factor* judge Cheryl Cole and Mariah Carey, who was a guest on the same night as Susan.

The song she was due to perform in front of the crowd was 'Wild Horses'. For most performers, this would involve a rush to the stylist, the salon and the gym, but here again Susan played it differently. She was spotted taking the 557 bus to nearby Bathgate where, surrounded by well-wishers, she posed for pictures and signed autographs. She then made her way to the local department store, M&Co, emerging an hour later with a bag full of new clothes. If she was turning into a diva, there were certainly no signs of it yet.

Her undiva-like behaviour nearly led to a disaster, though, when Susan dyed her hair an unfortunate shade of red. She didn't pay much heed to it until she arrived at the TV studios, but with only three hours to go before she was due to perform, emergency action was needed and a team of hairdressers was summoned to sort out the problem. A short while later, with her hair a more attractive darker shade of brown, Susan was ready to sing.

Her performance wasn't helped by the fact that she had developed a slight cough, and it was actually her second, utterly flawless take that ultimately made it to the screen. The audience didn't care, though: Susan got a standing ovation before she had so much as sung a note and a rapturous reception afterwards. It was 'bloody great' to be back, she said, adding, 'I feel great being back here, I feel at home and I loved performing. The public should watch out for the album.'

Presiding over it all, of course, was the ubiquitous Simon Cowell. Cowell has become, beyond a shadow of a doubt, the most influential person in British showbiz circles — and increasingly in American ones, too — and this was his moment. 'I feel so proud of you, and it's lovely to have you here,' he told Susan, but it was so much more than that. Without meaning to sound coy or cast aspersions, Simon was the fairy godmother here: it was he who had taken a shy little Scottish lady and transformed her into something quite different: a woman who was inspiring the world. In Susan he had picked the right person, for she had the talent to carry it off, but it was still Cowell who had facilitated her success and been the brains behind the most astonishing début the world had ever seen. This was Susan's *and* Simon's moment. Between the two of them, they were changing the face of musical history and redefining the limits of what could be achieved by whom. Shy little Susan had taken on the world, and with a little help from her friend Cowell, she had won.

Saturday, 11 April 2009. Britain was grouping around the nation's television sets, hunkering down to watch one of the most popular shows on TV, *Britain's Got Talent*. It was the first episode of the new series and no one had a clue what they were about to see that night.

In the theatre in Glasgow where the show was recorded, the three judges — Simon Cowell, Piers Morgan and the actress Amanda Holden — were seated at their desk. Behind them the audience roared with anticipation as each new act came on, with those roars frequently turning to derision as one act after another floundered, failing to live up to its promise. The mood soon turned to frank incredulity when a small, plump lady with unkempt grey hair, exuberant eyebrows and wearing an ill-fitting cream dress marched on to the stage, showing no discernable sign of being able to do anything very much. The cameras panned across the audience's faces: eyebrows were raised and bemused expressions seemed to be the order of the day. Who on earth was this? And how did she think she was going to justify being here tonight?

Simon, with his customary dispassionate sneer, took up pen and paper. 'Right,' he began, 'what's your name, darlin'?'

'My name is Susan Boyle,' replied the figure on the stage. She had a strong Scottish accent and there was a little nervous intake of breath, but otherwise she was calm.

'OK, er, Susan, where are you from?'

'I'm from Blackburn, near Bathgate, West Lothian.'

'It's a big town?'

'It's a sort of collection of, er, it's a collection,' Susan's hand circled desperately in the air, 'villages.' Her nerves were palpable now, but still under control. 'I had to think there!'

'And, how old are you, Susan?'

'I am forty-seven.' This provoked hoots and catcalls from the crowd, to which Susan responded with the hip wiggle that has become her trademark. 'And that's just one side of me,' she continued, wiggling more than ever. Piers wrinkled his nose in disbelief. 'What is this?' his expression seemed to say. Meanwhile, the camera panned to Ant and Dec, who were in hysterics backstage. 'I love it!' cried Ant, doing some wiggling himself.

Simon, by now wearing the expression of a weary schoolteacher faced with a couple of misbehaving nine-year-old boys, went on. 'Wow,' he said rather disapprovingly. 'OK, what's the dream?'

'I'm trying to be a professional singer,' replied Susan. That got a laugh from the audience, though not a sympathetic one, and more expressions of stunned disbelief flashed across the screen.

'And why hasn't it worked out so far, Susan?'

'I've never been given the chance before, but here's hoping it'll change,' said Susan with an expansive wave to the audience. Fat chance, they might have replied.

'OK, and who would you like to be as successful as?'

'Elaine Paige,' said Susan, prompting more calls from the audience who were definitely not on her side at this point.

'What are you going to sing tonight?' interjected Piers.

'I'm going to sing "I Dreamed A Dream" from *Les Miserables,*' said Susan to more hooting from the stalls. Amanda Holden looked suitably unimpressed.

'OK? It's on,' said Piers.

Susan turned to Ant and Dec on the side of the stage and gave them a thumbs-up. The music began to swell in the background and Susan brought the microphone to her mouth. She smiled — she, if no one else, knew what the audience was about to hear — then opened her mouth and out it came: 'I dreamed a dream in time gone by . . .'

The reaction was immediate: the audience exploded into cheers, and it was real cheering this time. Meanwhile the camera panned across the faces of the three judges, all of whom were registering amazement, shock and disbelief. On she went, causing the audience to get increasingly worked up.

'You didn't expect that now, did you? Did you? No,' Ant asked the camera as he and Dec looked stunned by what was happening on stage.

By this time Piers was clapping, Simon was beaming and the audience was getting to its feet to give Susan the first of several ovations she would receive over the course of her performance.

It was getting better and better out on stage. Susan's voice was soaring and she changed key without faltering, hitting the high notes and drawing out the full beauty of the song. Amanda was also on her feet applauding and Ant and Dec were chortling like naughty schoolboys. 'Look at that!' cried Ant. Look indeed.

Susan was beaming, totally in command of the stage and utterly different from the shy little woman who had walked out there. This was the voice of an astounding singer, and she finished to more rapturous applause and another standing ovation. As the music came to an end, Susan blew a kiss to the audience and began to walk from the stage.

This was not according to plan, and there was some pantomime action in the background as Ant and Dec motioned at her to go back. It was then that the full force of what had happened began to make itself felt.

'All right,' said Simon. 'Thank you very much, Susan. Piers?'

'Without a doubt that was the biggest surprise I have had in three years of this show,' Piers began. 'When you stood there with that cheeky grin and said, "I want to be like Elaine Paige," everyone was laughing at you. No one is laughing now. That was stunning. An incredible performance.' On stage, Susan was beaming. She was beginning to realize what had begun and blew out another kiss to the audience, who were eating out of her hand and roaring with delight.

'Amazing,' Piers continued. 'I'm reeling in shock. I don't know about you two.'

'I am so thrilled, because I know that everybody was against you,' said Amanda bluntly. 'I honestly think that we were all being very cynical and I think that's the biggest wake-up call ever, and I just want to say that it was a complete privilege listening to that. It was inspirational.' The audience burst out into yet another round of applause.

'Thank you very much,' Susan replied.

Simon couldn't help playing the joker. 'I knew the minute you walked out on that stage that we were going to hear something extraordinary, and I was right,' he said, to laughter from the audience and an admonishment of, 'Oh, Simon!' from Susan herself.

'What a lot of tosh!' cried Dec.

'Susan,' Simon continued, 'you are a little tiger, aren't you?'

'I don't know about that,' said Susan.

'You are. OK, moment of truth. Yes or no?'

'The biggest yes I have ever given anybody,' said Piers as Susan began to laugh in amazed delight.

'Amanda?'

'Yes, definitely.' Susan was beginning to look a little stunned now.

'Susan Boyle,' said Simon, 'you can go back to the village with your head held high, with three yeses.'

Susan couldn't contain herself. She shook her fists in the air, did a little victory dance on the spot and finally left the stage, blowing one last kiss to an audience which was on its feet again. It had not only been one of the most extraordinary moments on a televised talent show, but one of the most extraordinary moments ever on a television screen.

Susan had had a little chat with Ant and Dec prior to going on stage, so the viewer at home was quite as bemused as everyone in the studio by what they were seeing. Chatting to the two of them, Susan confessed she was nearly forty-eight, that she had a cat called Pebbles and had never been married or kissed, a comment she would come to regret in the fullness of time given the amount of media attention it garnered. She came across as an awkward little thing, confessing to nerves, but wanting to get out there and give it her all. And then, of course, she did just that.

'I'm going to make that audience rock,'

she told Ant and Dec, who looked as if they wouldn't count on it, but were far too polite to say so.

The reaction in the next day's papers was similarly astonished. That such a stunning voice could come from someone who wasn't groomed to within an inch of her life was greeted with sheer disbelief: 'She has a soaring, beautiful voice that could grace a heavenly choir — but self-taught singer Susan Boyle has the hair-do from hell,' proclaimed Mark Jefferies in the *Mirror*. 'And the scruffy 47-year-old stunned judges on *Britain's Got Talent* when she opened her mouth and produced "the biggest surprise ever" on the show.'

He called it a 'stunning performance' and he was not alone. The *Daily Telegraph* called her a 'singing marvel', the *Daily Star* reported how the audience was 'stunned' by her 'amazing' voice, and the *Sunday Express* commented on her 'electrifying performance'. More amazingly still, the sort of people who wouldn't normally have noticed a lady of a certain age giving it her all in a moment that would change her life joined in. The Hollywood star Demi Moore tweeted that it was one of the most moving things she had ever seen and Oprah Winfrey wanted her on the show. A clip of the audition found its way on to YouTube, where it promptly became — and still is — the hottest thing online. At the time of writing, it had received over 35 million hits on that channel and well over three times that worldwide.

The interest in Susan was immediate and intense, provoked by the contrast in her appearance and her voice. On the one hand she was being compared to Paul Potts, another ungainly looking singer who had won *Britain's Got Talent* two years earlier thanks to his remarkable voice, but the reaction Susan provoked was quite unique. It was inconceivable. Nothing like that had ever happened before.

But though the world of television was reeling, it was nothing compared to what Susan was feeling. Being thrust into the public eye like this would have given even the most savvy media manipulator pause for thought. But Susan wasn't savvy: what you saw was exactly what you got, and so, having no concept of how huge the interest in her was, or how everything she said and did would be magnified by the unforgiving glare of the newspapers (with the possible exception of the *Financial Times*), Susan made various remarks and jokes that got blown up out of all proportion. At this early stage she had minimum guidance on how to deal with the press, for the simple reason that no one had anticipated the level of interest she received.

An early case in point was an off-the-cuff remark Susan made about Piers Morgan, for whom she undoubtedly developed a tendresse, but not quite to the extent that it was written up in some quarters. She had already confessed live on air that she had 'never been kissed', although even that was not quite the truth, and now, rather unwisely, she spoke of her admiration for Piers.

'Up until now I have never met the right man, but maybe that will change now I have met Piers,' she declared to the bevy of reporters who had gathered outside her modest home in Blackburn, anxiously digging up every bit of information about this extraordinary woman who had so enthralled the nation. 'He's a very handsome man. It's quite hard to choose between Piers and Simon because they're both lovely, but I think it would definitely be Piers.'

It was pretty harmless stuff, but a gift to the writers of the huge amounts of copy that would come to be written about SuBo, as she came to be nicknamed.

However, there was also a more serious side to what Susan had to tell the reporters who trailed her. It wasn't just that she was casual about her appearance and a bit of a country bumpkin, she'd had genuine medical difficulties that had caused her problems all her life. Without a hint of self-pity Susan declared, 'I am a slow learner. All my life people have told me what I can't do rather than what I can do, so it's nice to show the country that I can sing. I find it so much easier than talking to people. I sing from the heart and can communicate how I feel so much easier.'

That wasn't the end of it, either. While Susan wasn't a creature to be pitied, her life had clearly been harsh, not least because she lived alone. 'I lived with my mum up until she died two years ago from old age,' she went on. 'Now I only have my cat Pebbles for company, but when I sing I know my mum is still listening.'

As all this and more came out, the atmosphere surrounding Susan shifted. When she'd first walked out on to that Glasgow stage there had been an unmistakable sense of mockery in the air; a feeling that an ungroomed woman from the sticks who compared herself to Elaine Paige was setting herself up for a fall. But as Susan's vulnerabilities became clear, there was a pervading sense of shame about people's initial reactions. Susan had clearly been bullied all her life in one form or another, and now here she was, having the guts to stand up in front of 3,000 people in an auditorium, 11 million on television and, courtesy of You-Tube, 33 million worldwide and show what she could do. Why shouldn't this woman be given a chance? Why shouldn't she be allowed to achieve her full potential? And above all, what right had others to mock? She was only human. Didn't she have feelings, too?

Nor did it seem right to be unkind about someone who had led such an exceptionally sheltered life. 'I've never been kissed,' she reiterated to the *Mirror* as the newspapers fought with one another to see who could get her life story first. 'If someone even pecked me on the cheek it would be nice, but I've never even got that close. My parents didn't want me to have boyfriends so I've never been on a date. I suppose I've accepted it's never going to happen. The only thing I really do regret is not having children. I love kids and would have liked to have been a mum.'

That crush on Piers — whose long-term girlfriend is the journalist Celia Walden — was making itself felt, too. 'He's gorgeous,' Susan repeated. 'I remember when *Ameri-*

ca's Got Talent first came on and I saw him and thought, He looks really nice, I wonder who he is? I was too embarrassed to tell him how I felt when I was at my audition, but I had my hair curled especially for the show and wore a dress I'd bought a few months back for my nephew's wedding. I like Simon Cowell, too. He is beautiful but he's the boss. I've got too much respect for him to have feelings like that. I used to have a crush on Terry Wogan, too, but he's a bit old for me now.'

No one with a heart who heard any of this could have failed to feel for Susan. Although it was later to emerge that she had been on television once before and had had at least one suitor, her sheer artlessness as she described her background and life was as powerful as anything she said. There was no agenda here; it was quite simple. Susan wanted to be a singer, had never had any real opportunities before and was taking advantage of getting noticed any way she could. She was a modest, straightforward woman who had nursed her mother in old age and who lived alone with her cat. Who could fail to be moved by that?

It was all of these elements — Susan's modesty, lack of self-pity, dignity in the face of bereavement and bullying and, of course, her beautiful voice — that made it clear early on that she would become a sensation. Furthermore, she was attracting a huge amount of attention in the United States. As well as *Oprah,* a string of American talk shows and channels had expressed an interest in her, including *Larry King Live, Good Morning America,* NBC and CBS.

Meanwhile Elaine Paige, who had noted Susan's ambition to emulate her own success, promptly provided her with another celebrity endorsement. Indeed, she went a step further by suggesting they work together. 'Ever since Susan's appearance on *Britain's Got Talent* my Radio 2 inbox has been flooded with emails,' she wrote on her website. 'It seems her performance has captured the hearts of everyone who saw it, me included . . . it looks like I have competition! Perhaps we should record a duet? She is a role model for everyone who has a dream.'

Sir Cameron Mackintosh, who staged the original production of *Les Miserables,* agreed. 'I think there's every chance Susan Boyle will have the number one album in America, I will predict that,' he said. 'I was gobsmacked by her powerhouse performance. Vocally it was one of the best versions of the song I've ever heard.' Sir Cameron is one of the most influential people in British theatre, and has worked with some of its biggest names, so coming from him this was high praise indeed.

Susan duly appeared on *Larry King Live*, along with Piers Morgan, who asked her out to dinner (an invitation she accepted). During the interview Susan tried to make sense of the extraordinary events of the previous few days. 'It's all been complete mayhem, like a whirlwind going on an express train,' she said. 'I never expected all this attention. It's been indescribable and completely mad, but I could get used to it.'

Piers Morgan was staggered by everything that was happening to Susan and was one of the first to see her huge potential and the massive possibilities for this extraordinary new find. Like many of the people involved in *Britain's Got Talent* and Susan's life, Piers blogged regularly, and at the time he wrote, 'I can remember the moment she first opened her lips perfectly,' he wrote. 'I can honestly say it was one of the most extraordinary moments in my perhaps equally unlikely career as a talent show judge. Susan Boyle is not just a good singer, she's a fantastic singer. As I watched her performance back again I texted to Simon in Hollywood: "My God, Susan was even bet-

ter than I remembered. She's unbelievable."
He agreed, and I could almost feel his beady
little eyes going "KERCHING!" down the
line. For unless I am a brainless aardvark
then this West Lothian villager is going to
sell a lot of records once this series is over.'

Even at this early stage, with only one appearance on *Britain's Got Talent* behind her,
and before anyone had a clue how things
were going to pan out, there was talk of an
album. No one yet knew what a phenomenon Susan was to become, but industry
insiders knew they'd seen something special,
and were keenly aware of her commercial
potential. Larry King put this to her, but
Susan wisely played it down.

'It's too early for things like that,' she said.
'I'm just taking baby steps until I see how I
do in the competition.' Nor, as yet, did she
see any need to change her appearance.
'Why should I change?' she asked. She was
to change her mind on that one, however,
and pretty soon, too.

Indeed, in another interview Susan gave
back then — and she was inundated with
requests — she seemed less happy with how
she'd come across. 'They say that television
makes you look fat and it certainly did,' she
told the *Mirror*. 'I looked like a garage. It
was mortifying to see and a bit of a shock. I

51

didn't realize I could reduce people to tears and I hope it wasn't because of that. I'm proud to be part of the show. It really is a dream come true.'

How much of a dream was brought home to her when she attended the Easter service at her local Catholic church and was greeted by a standing ovation — something she would get used to in the months ahead. She had worked in the church as a volunteer for years, but now suddenly the tables were turned and the congregation was applauding her. 'It was incredible,' said Susan afterwards. 'Although we sing in church, not a lot of them knew how good I was, so it was a bit of a shock to them. I'm a bit shy and retiring so they would never have known. It was very emotional. Everyone is very nice and it's lovely when all the kids stop me in the street to congratulate me.'

That was a change, too. Although Susan was well liked in the village, there was a rogue element that made life difficult for her, and they were certainly learning to look at her in a very different way. 'People used to shout things at her in the street, but they have all changed their tune now,' said Vicky McLean, one of Susan's neighbours. 'I ran into her the other day on the way to the shops and she said she knew who her real friends were — the people who liked her before the show. She knows that a lot of the people calling round now are not being genuine.'

Vicky was not alone in feeling some concern, but although people's fears were to prove well grounded, plenty of well-wishers were keen to point out that Susan had had a difficult life to date and that this, no matter what problems might come in its wake, was a way to a happier life. Catherine Hunter, a neighbour who has known Susan since childhood, was one of them. 'It had been Susan's dream to try out for *Britain's Got Talent*,' she told the *Daily Express*. 'She used to watch it with her mum Bridget, whom she lived with and cared for until she died two years ago at the age of ninety-one.

'They used to watch the show and her mum encouraged her to go on it. But after she died Susan stopped singing and became very depressed. This has really helped her confidence. Her mother and father, who died some time ago, would be proud. We all are. Last Saturday night the whole street turned out to wish her well after the programme ended. All the doors opened and everyone piled out shouting congratulations to her.'

Another lifelong friend, Elain Clarke, was

more concerned. 'Susan is shy around people she doesn't know until she sings — and then she loves an audience,' she said. 'She is well known in the village for her beautiful voice and sings regularly at the pub. She sings all the time, and when she has the windows open we can hear her all over the street. When we have barbecues in the summer she goes from garden to garden singing. She's safe here in this village but she needs to be properly managed with all this success. I hope she's looked after.' It was a concern that was to raise its head again and again.

While some people around Susan might not have been genuine, the excitement surrounding her was palpable. The clip of her audition on YouTube was getting millions of hits, as the story of this slightly dowdy woman with the extraordinary voice spread across the world. Susan continued to protest that she wouldn't change her appearance, or indeed anything else, and that it was her singing that was important. Amanda Holden joined in, urging Susan not to change. Everyone had a view on some aspect of Susan's life and everyone wanted to contribute to the debate. But the juggernaut that had roared into action was now going too fast for Susan, or anyone else, to control.

■ ■ ■ ■

Since her first appearance, it had been established that her father was a soldier and that she was one of nine children, who were all thrilled for their sister, if a little concerned that her success might get out of hand.

Her brother John said, 'The reaction Susan is getting is just amazing. She is long overdue this recognition.' And it was thrilling, not least because Susan herself was so totally overwhelmed by what was happening. The title of the song she sang to get her into her current position couldn't have been more apposite. She'd dreamed a dream, all right — and now it seemed that dream was coming true.

In interviews, Susan had very publicly made it known that she was a virgin, and now men were letting it be known that they'd be happy to do something about this if she so wished. 'I'm flattered and delighted by the attention,' said Susan, wisely leaving it at that.

It was now that the term 'Hairy Angel' was coined, a description that Susan was none too keen on and which might have played a part in persuading her to get a makeover. The YouTube footage of her interview continued to astound: within five days of the performance, it had had 20 million hits, six times more than that achieved by Britney Spears.

It wasn't just Larry King who had lured Susan on to his show either. At home in Blackburn television crews from all over the world were seen arriving to interview her. Diane Sawyer, another of America's top presenters, had her on as a guest, and so did almost everyone, and those that didn't were still aware of who she was and what she'd done. In a sign of America's growing fascination with Susan, Jay Leno, another hugely popular talk show host, dressed up as her in a gold dress and wig. 'My mother was Scottish, she came from the same part of Scotland and I think we are related,' he told his cheering audience. 'When you saw her sing, did you see any resemblance?'

Susan somehow managed to enjoy it and have a good time. 'I can't believe how lucky I am,' she told the *Daily Express*. 'Keep them coming is what I say. I'm amazed that these TV stations from all over the world have come to see me. I haven't taken it in completely and most mornings I wake up with a smile on my face because I can't believe it has happened. It's overwhelming and I am enjoying it but I'm keeping my feet firmly on the ground.'

Everyone wanted a piece of her. Russell Brand, that noted lothario, quipped, 'Susan has pledged to lose her virginity to the winner of a breakdancing showdown between me and her eyebrow. I must win!'

Piers Morgan chipped in, 'Susan, if you're listening — I'm available! I've decided to extend an invitation to Susan to take her for a meal at a romantic restaurant. Maybe some roses, fine wine, glamorous waiters and the chance to break her kissing duck with me.'

Was that going too far? Piers was, and remains, one of Susan's most stalwart supporters, but it's possible he, like everyone else, was getting carried away with the moment. Certainly, concerns were mounting in some quarters that even a robust individual would have trouble coping with this level of attention, let alone someone as vulnerable as Susan. Despite the fact that Susan's learning disabilities were well known, the full extent of her fragility had not become evident. In a matter of days, Susan had gone from being completely unknown to one of the most famous people on the planet. Her family stepped in, rallied round and, for a while, Susan went into hiding to give everyone a chance to calm down and get back to normal. But however much she hid away, there was no denying that her life had changed beyond all recognition — and in only a week.

Desperately Seeking Susan

Susan Boyle was an absolute sensation, there was no doubt about that. Some cynics had thought that after the initial flurry of interest the nation would forget all about her, as had happened to so many reality TV stars before her, but quite the opposite appeared to be true. The public's fascination with Susan grew and grew, and not just among people who liked musical theatre, either. The young, cool and trendy were as taken with this Scottish lady of a certain age as anyone else, and nowhere was this exemplified more than by the now famous tweets from Demi Moore and her husband Ashton Kutcher.

'This just made my night,' tweeted Ashton.

'You saw it made me teary,' Demi replied. Meanwhile, fresh from making jokes about her, Russell Brand popped up again, this time on a surprisingly serious note. 'I just watched Susan Boyle for the first time and it's very moving to see latent talent realized,' he wrote. If ever there was an indication of the impact Susan had made on the nation, it was that. It's impossible to think of two more disparate characters than Russell Brand and Susan Boyle, and yet she'd won him over, too.

Susan herself stayed out of the picture. Wisely, she allowed the furore to rage on whilst she got used to the fact that, having been plucked from total obscurity, she had become one of the most famous people on earth. And although none of this had been planned — even Simon Cowell would have had a problem choreographing this one — the way events panned out only served to fuel the interest in her.

While ducking out of sight came out of necessity rather than calculation, the truth is that you always want what you can't have, and the public wanted Susan. And when they couldn't have her, they wanted her even more. Susan wasn't due to reappear on the show until the following month, which in turn allowed expectation, interest and anticipation to build around her. All the while details about Susan's life contin-ued to emerge in dribs and drabs, as report-ers besieged the village of Blackburn, desperate to find out anything they could about her. The picture that emerged was of a good woman, who had suffered both as a child and more recently. The death of her mother had affected her badly, on top of which, a yob element in the village had occasionally made life even more difficult for her.

There was certainly no shortage of neighbours willing to speak up on her behalf. One such was Brian Smith, who had known her for years and was extremely keen to refute the notion that Susan had never been kissed.

'She's been through difficult and very low times in the past few years. She's a lovely lady, really kind and generous. She would make a great catch for any man,' he told the *Mirror,* and it was testament to Susan's kind heart that she provoked such effusive outbursts. 'It's not true Susan's never been kissed,' he went on. 'I've given her many a peck on the cheek to say, "Don't worry, everything's going to be all right." She comes to me when she needs help or a shoulder to cry on.'

It turned out that Susan, like so many single women, had become the primary carer for her mother Bridget, and Bridget's death three years earlier had left a terrible gap in her life. It was doubtless difficult while Bridget was alive, but times became even harder after she died. In short, Susan hadn't really had a lot of fun in her life.

'I never knew her to have a birthday party because she was busy caring for her mother,' Brian continued. 'When she was left alone in that house she went through extremely down times. She wouldn't come out for three or four days or answer the door or phone.'

Nor were matters helped by local youths. 'They would call her names, throw snowballs at her door and dare each other to knock and run away,' said Brian. 'She would confront them and get really angry, which made them ridicule her more. We'd often chase them away.'

With a background like that, Susan's bravery about facing the Glasgow audience on *Britain's Got Talent* was becoming more understandable by the day. She had been taunted, bullied and humiliated in the past, and had she not carried off such a spectacular performance, there was a very good chance it would have happened again, except this time on national television. While much was made of Susan's learning difficulties, you couldn't fault her ambition. She'd seen that this was one way of achieving her dream and she'd gone for it. And so far it was working out spectacularly well.

You couldn't have a voice like Susan's without somebody noticing, and so it proved to be. It turned out that Susan was a regular at karaoke contests held at the local Happy Valley Hotel, where her talent hadn't gone unobserved. 'Susan comes here three or four times a week, although you wouldn't notice her,' the hotel's owner Jackie Russell told the *Mirror*. 'She sits by herself with a glass of lemonade. Then she sees the microphone and you definitely notice her.'

In the meantime, public concern at the patronizing way this gentle woman had been treated by the *Britain's Got Talent* judges had filtered through to the hard-boiled trio, and Piers and Amanda apologized for the way they'd been on the show (and for those remarks about making up for her lack of male attention — Piers really should have said sorry for a great deal more).

'I would just like to apologize to Susan, it's long overdue,' he said. 'Simon Cowell and I don't have the best reputations, I think, for courtesy. We were all laughing at her when she started, but she had the last laugh. It was an amazing performance.'

Amanda hadn't been much better: 'It's a very shallow thing to say, but obviously the minute she walked on we and the audience completely judged her on her appearance,' she said, 'and I hate saying that. The audience was jeering and booing and it was really uncomfortable. And we were, "Oh, just please be good or just get off." We were so dying for her.' But then, as Amanda put it, everyone cottoned on to the fact that they'd 'found gold'.

If truth be told, this was a bit rich coming from Piers and Amanda, especially Amanda, who had repeatedly told Susan not to change, not to smarten up and not to go to Simon Cowell's dentist . . . The observant among us will have noted that Amanda isn't exactly a stranger to the beauty salon herself. Although Susan was, perhaps for the first time in her life, being taken seriously in some quarters, there were still a great number of patronizing comments coming her way simply because she wasn't a city-dwelling sophisticate. The bullies in the village may have been silenced, but the cattiness in the media would linger for some time yet.

Given the level of interest Susan's appearance had provoked, when the next episode of *Britain's Got Talent* aired the following week, expectation was huge. In the end, nothing particularly dramatic happened: a twelve-year-old called Shaheen Jafargholi got the Cowell treatment when Simon stopped him halfway through Amy Winehouse's 'Valerie' and got him to perform another number, Michael Jackson's 'Who's Loving You', which turned out to be a huge triumph and caused the other judges to give him a pat on the back.

Then Amanda was reduced to tears (again) by a saxophonist called Julian Smith . . . and so it went on. There was talent there, certainly, but nothing to produce a show-stopping moment à la Susan. How could there have been? What had happened to Susan was a one-in-a-million TV moment, and even though she was physically absent from the show, her presence hung over it. For Susan, who had been ritually ignored for years when she was around, the fact that she could cast a spell in her absence was as thrilling as being finally accepted as a singer.

Still no one knew quite where Susan was — not that it stopped various lurid reports from surfacing. That never-been-kissed tag was still there (a peck on the cheek wasn't really deemed sufficient) and so a friend, William McDonald, stepped forward to do the honours. 'If there's a lady to be kissed, I'm your man,' he explained, adding, 'She'd be looking for a younger fellow now she's world famous.' Perhaps, but she wasn't going to have time. It seemed everyone wanted a piece of Susan, and remaining in the shadows just made everyone want her all the more.

The second episode of the show only served to crank up the dramatic tension. Despite the strength of Susan's performance, and the sensation it had provoked, it was by no means a given that Susan would win, and it appeared she had serious competition in the form of Shaheen. Their rivalry was being billed as the Hairy Angel versus the Little Angel, with even Michael Jackson expressing an interest in meeting the youngster when he visited London to perform that summer (poignantly, Shaheen later ended up performing at Jackson's memorial service).

Shaheen, to put it bluntly, also had a good back story: the son of a single mother, he was a little lad with a big voice that he used to full effect. He was also only twelve, and thus as ill-equipped to deal with the pressures of televisual fame as Susan, not least because the media were keen to set them up against one another.

'Susan has an amazing voice,' said Shaheen, who was nothing if not diplomatic. 'I don't want to be a rival, but if I won I wouldn't be complaining. I know I am a good singer and I think I can sing as well as anyone else in the competition. I enjoy doing it so much.'

'Susan and Shaheen are very different singers,' his mother Karen chipped in. 'If it comes down to it, may the best person win on the night.'

Unlike Susan, Shaheen already had some professional experience. He had appeared in *Torchwood* and *Casualty,* and had toured with the musical *Thriller,* in which he played the young Michael Jackson. But it seemed that Susan's amateurishness didn't matter: it was all part of her charm.

Even without the discovery of Susan and the rivalry between her and Shaheen, this series of *Britain's Got Talent* was getting a lot of attention. Simon Cowell made headlines when he appointed a fourth judge, the actress Kelly Brook, and then made even more headlines when he dispensed with her services just two days into filming. Cowell said her presence upset the dynamic of the show, while Kelly herself claimed that Ant and Dec had been behind it, partly because they were angry not to have been consulted and partly because she unwisely asked them what they did!

All the while, though, Susan's story continued to fascinate. The next snippet about her life that came to light was that shortly before she appeared on television, Susan applied to join the Cantilena Choir in Livingston, West Lothian, but had been turned down. 'She made an enquiry to join our choir, but we had no vacancies,' explained Shirley Ullman, the choir secretary. 'When she spoke to me she had just done the audition for *Britain's Got Talent*. It was a shock when I saw her on the television. We are a very small choir so we didn't want to be top heavy. There are only eighteen of us and we are more of a chamber choir rather than there being fifty to sixty people, so we just couldn't have too many singers.' On this occasion, however, they would seem to have been the ones missing out.

Talk continued about a record deal, and as fans and journalists began visiting Blackburn to get a glimpse of the unlikely new star, Susan, who had resurfaced, was forced to put a wall up at her house to shield herself from the curious gaze of the public.

Meanwhile, Boyle-mania continued to grow. It emerged that as far back as 1999, Susan had sung 'Cry Me A River' on a record made for charity — a very rare disc, as only 1,000 had ever been made — and one had now surfaced on eBay, attracting bids reaching as high as £1,000.

Hugh Jackman, star of the X-Men film series, became the latest Hollywood star to declare himself a fan. 'Where is Susan Boyle?' he tweeted. 'I am ready for a duet.' This wasn't as outlandish a request as it seemed since Hugh is in fact a musical talent in his own right, having starred in a concert version of *Carousel* at New York's Carnegie Hall. And while Alain Boublil might not be as well known as some of the other names speaking about Susan, he certainly knows a thing or two about music, having written the lyrics for 'I Dreamed A Dream'. 'I think of Edith Piaf,' he said. 'Piaf was a small woman who looked like nothing, and then she opened her mouth and this beautiful sound came out. Even the most cynical people I know have been moved.' Elaine Paige and now Edith Piaf — high praise indeed.

Meanwhile, Susan's audition continued to become one of the most viewed in the history of the internet, with over 100 million hits: 'There have been moments in the history of viral video when it seems as if the whole world unites around one phenomenon,' declared Matt Cutler, a spokesman for the American video tracking company Visible Measures. 'The latest star is the unassuming, unexpectedly talented Susan Boyle. The humble and previously unknown Susan Boyle in less than one week has trumped everyone.'

Shortly afterwards the number rose to 116 million. 'She is very close to becoming the most popular internet hit in history,' Cutler said. 'We are watching closely and counting how many people are logging in on over 150 websites, not just YouTube.'

Susan had started to appear in public again, and for the first time there was the hint of a change in her appearance. Her hair, although still grey, had been trimmed, and her clothes were starting to appear a little smarter. Susan had been adamant that there would be no Hollywood-style make-over, but anyone who appears regularly on television is aware of their appearance, and Susan, while not yet a regular performer, had attracted more attention than almost anyone else on the planet. It was hardly surprising that, despite Amanda's rather patronizing plea that Susan stay the way she was, a slight change began to occur.

Susan even acknowledged as much. 'I will need to sort out my dress sense and my weight,' she told one of the numerous journalists who hung on her every word. 'It wasn't until I saw myself on TV that I realized how frumpy I was. It's not a big thing, it doesn't worry me too much, but I will be doing a bit more exercise to help me sort it out.

'When there is this much attention on you, you have to plan what you wear every day and look your best. I just want to look nice and smart.' It was a typically modest assertion and didn't suggest anything too extreme.

By now, Susan was beginning to get offers to make a record, which she duly turned down. Under the terms of *Britain's Got Talent,* she was not allowed to sign up with anyone else, but she was also aware that it was too soon. The video clip of her audition might have been a sensation, but the fact remained that she had been on the show only once. She had to go back, prove it wasn't a one-off and that she could take the pace. She was also going to need professional help. No industry has more sharks than the music industry, and Susan had become a highly marketable commodity. As such she was going to need people around to protect her from making a bad deal.

Susan certainly hadn't seen a penny yet. By this stage in any series of *Britain's Got Talent,* none of the contestants would have earned a thing, but Susan found herself in that odd space between the very famous and the very rich. While she was certainly becoming the former, she was nowhere near the latter. She had the *Britain's Got Talent* team to look after her — although it wasn't yet clear quite how much she was going to need it — but she had no money to lavish on makeovers and security. She was already in an extremely pressurized position and this just added to everything she had to worry about.

The internet hits reached 130 million, at least 80 million more than the viewings for President Obama's inauguration speech. 'I am truly gobsmacked,' said Susan. 'This is unbelievable. The reaction has been amazing.' She celebrated by having a slight eyebrow trim — an altogether sleeker Susan was beginning to emerge.

And still the celebrity endorsements continued. It seemed as though the most famous and blessed people on the planet wanted to be sprinkled with the gold dust that had transformed Susan's life.

'She gave me the chill bumps when I heard her,' said Sheryl Crow.

'I got emailed the link and was most impressed,' said Billy Zane. 'I enjoyed the comeuppance the audience got. It was a milestone in compassion.'

'My fifteen-year-old son said, "That makes me so happy," ' said Anthony Edwards.

The performance was 'warm and friendly', said Sidney Poitier.

Even Tony Blair got in on the act: 'Susan is certainly unofficially probably doing more good than most of the official channels of diplomacy,' he said. And where Blair was to be found, so was his erstwhile spin doctor, Alistair Campbell, who thought politicians could take a leaf out of Susan's book: it was her authenticity, he said, that made her such a success.

Someone else touched by Susan's gold dust was Amanda Holden. She was, of course, on the audition clip that had been beamed all over the world, and in the wake of that, Amanda had been interviewed innumerable times about Susan, not least on American television. It seemed the Americans liked what they saw, and why not? Simon and Piers were stars in the States, so why not Amanda?

She had certainly been keen on the idea in the past, saying, 'I want that for myself. I bloody well would like to go over there.' And now it seemed she was going to get the chance. CBS offered her a job co-anchoring *The Early Show* after *Britain's Got Talent* finished on 30 May — and all because of the worldwide interested generated by Susan. It all served to enhance the fairytale quality of the story — not only had Susan's life changed, everyone around her was experiencing good fortune too.

Amanda continued to emphasize that Susan shouldn't change, however. 'Everyone was against Susan when she walked on that stage,' she told the American audience. 'We all were. We were all too cynical. It was a complete privilege to listen to Susan, but she needs to stay exactly as she is, because that's the reason we love her. A makeover can perhaps come later, when she's signed the album deal and conquered America.' In actual fact, the makeover had already begun.

Susan's changing appearance was, in reality, a physical manifestation of her change in status. No one had taken her seriously before, but they were now, and as her popularity grew, so she came closer to the commonly held ideal of what makes a woman attractive. However much Amanda and co. might have wanted Susan to stay the same, the fact remained that Susan *wanted* to change.

She had never been allowed to feel that she could compete with the rest of the world on any basis, be it as a sexually attractive woman or a person who could have an interesting life in her own right. Until now she had been daughter, sister, aunt, carer, and not a great deal more. Cinderella, to whom she was increasingly compared, rose from the ashes to don her finery, and metaphorically, Susan was doing exactly the same.

Meanwhile Susan's makeover was gradually taking place. Her eyebrows were noticeably slimmer, her hair had been trimmed and now it went from grey to auburn. Susan's wardrobe underwent a similar metamorphosis when she was pictured wearing smart trousers and a light brown jacket, an outfit that was a world away from her appearance a week earlier.

All this time, it was increasingly apparent that in private her voice had been stunning family and friends for years.

The *Mirror* unearthed an old family video of Susan singing 'I Don't Know How To Love Him' from the musical *Jesus Christ Superstar* when she was just twenty-five. 'It was a very emotional night,' her brother Gerry told the paper. 'It goes quiet when Susan sings; it always does. She always has that effect. The week before she went on *Britain's Got Talent* she sang "Ave Maria" at my mother-in-law's funeral and stunned the church.'

Extraordinary aspects of Susan's story just kept emerging. It turned out the Boyle family, or at least some elements of it, were moving in rather higher echelons than had been previously suspected, as none other than Sir David Frost was a friend. He had met Gerry, and another brother John, twenty years previously, when the brothers suggested setting up a property firm based on Sir David's television show *Through The Keyhole.*

'We're still friends with him and he gets in touch regularly,' said John, who also lives in Blackburn. 'He will definitely be in touch when he realizes what Susan is doing. That's just the kind of guy he is.' Indeed, David had been one of the first to call the family after their mother Bridget died two years earlier.

Susan's appearance continued to change subtly, with every new brush of lipstick being excitedly reported by the press, not to mention her first outing in heels and a sleekly fashionable pashmina.

In many ways, Susan was going through what most women do in their teens: learning how to use make-up, finding out what suited her and what didn't, experimenting with new hairdos and having fun. And why shouldn't she? Susan's life had been tough so far, but as the writer George Eliot once said, 'It's never too late to be what you might have been.'

It wasn't long before the real experts in their fields were hauled in. Nicky Clarke, the celebrity hairdresser, had a consultation with Susan, and while his assessment of her was a little cruel, he could certainly see potential. 'At the moment she looks a bit like a man in drag, but there's a lot of potential there, and when I'm finished she is going to look really beautiful,' he said. 'I'm going to soften her hair with low-lights, which will freshen the face up. She will look stunning.' The duckling was turning into a swan.

It was only two weeks into the new series, but although Susan was clearly a hot favourite to win, there were plenty of cynics who felt sure that Cowell and co. had a few tricks up their sleeves, and the latest sensation to be pulled out of the bag was Hollie Steel, a ten-year-old child with a fine singing voice. She, too, had a story to tell, in her case a serious bout of pneumonia when she was four that nearly resulted in losing a lung when she was treated in The Royal

Manchester Children's Hospital.

'She was in hospital for three months and there were moments when it was life and death — she was all skin and bones and doctors thought she might not recover,' her mother Nina said. 'Even when she stabilized, they told me they would have to remove a lung. I was in bits and at times thought she might not make it, or if she did, she wouldn't be able to lead a normal life. Now she has this amazing voice that melts your heart — it's a miracle she can sing at all.

'They told us they would have to remove a lung and that if that was the case it would lead to curvature of the spine and muscles around the heart twisting as she grew, because there would be nothing supporting her side,' Nina continued. 'She had two major operations to save her lung and thankfully started responding to antibiotics. When she first started singing she had this powerful voice on her and I asked a specialist singing teacher to check her out in case it was dangerous after all that had happened to her. But luckily they said she was fine. I love to listen to them [Hollie and her brother Joshua] both sing; it makes me so proud.'

This was what Susan was up against, not

just in terms of talent, but in how much human interest the stories could provide. But however much stories about brave youngsters battling illness might have filled the papers, there was nothing to compare to her. Susan's story wasn't only inspiring, it was moving: it gave hope to every person who felt they had lost out in life's lottery and who hoped that one day their fortunes would change. Susan was proof it could be done.

In the background, however, ructions were beginning to emerge. Susan's family, while delighted about her success, were becoming concerned about the pressure she was under, and were worried that she wouldn't be able to cope. There was talk of taking her away to the United States to escape all the commotion, while her brother Gerry, perhaps unwisely, claimed she was now 'too big' for *Britain's Got Talent*. 'If Susan isn't removed or eliminated there's going to be a riot in the street,' he told the *Irish Sunday Mirror*. 'There is a public appetite for a single but no product for people to buy. *BGT* need to step in and sort this out. The silence coming from *BGT* is causing a frenzy. We are all getting sucked into it and it's getting a bit much now.'

Then there was Susan's mental state. 'When I last spoke to Susan she sounded exhausted,' Gerry continued. 'I said, "How are you?" and she said, "Oh, Gerard, I've been here, there and everywhere." She's been up and down to London for meetings with Sony. I could tell she was shattered. I said to her, "Get off the phone and get to bed. You need to rest." Susan is frustrated. She's not thinking about big cars and Bentleys. All she wants to do is sing, but she's not being allowed to do that. The pressure would be much less, and the whole thing much better, if there was a management team to look after her.'

What Gerard didn't seem to take on board was that Susan's silence was building up expectations even more. No one yet knew if this was a one-off or whether she would be able to carry it through, and while it was putting enormous pressure on Susan's shoulders, it was also setting up a situation in which she would prosper if she pulled it off, though if she didn't it would all come to nought — but that's showbusiness. Ultimately, if she was to have the career she wanted, she would have to be able to cope with the downsides, too.

Gerry was also concerned about the huge press attention Susan was receiving. 'I have stayed away from what used to be our family house because there are so many people camped out there,' he said. 'It's been like a scene from the film *Notting Hill* every time she opens the front door. I know Susan thinks she's staying in that house to her dying day, but someone needs to step in and do what's right for her. Is there a management deal or not? I imagined Cowell would move forward on this. But she's got too big for the show. I understand Cowell wants to protect his show, but they can't have their cake and eat it. Everyone wants to know why Susan isn't going to America and why there isn't a CD in the shops. They want to keep her solely in their eyes as a contestant on *Britain's Got Talent.* But the time for keeping her within the confines of *Britain's Got Talent* has passed. This isn't working.'

If Gerry was deliberately trying to rile Cowell, he couldn't have done a better job, and this wasn't an end to it. 'We've got a star on our hands and the appetite for her first record is huge,' Gerry continued. 'From a business point of view they are not capitalizing on her success. Any established act would love to crack America, but Susan's done it in eight days. So do we keep on going and take up these offers or — for the good of the show — do we ignore the fact everyone is baying for a product? They can't just sit back and ignore this phenomenon just because she's a contestant.' In actual fact, the last thing they were doing was ignoring Susan, and Gerry's comments weren't helping matters at all.

It was certainly true that Susan was feeling the full glare of the media in a way that few people have to cope with, and that she had neither the experience nor the cynicism to deal with it. There was a permanent encampment of journalists and camera crews outside her front door, while her every move was monitored, analysed and examined under the media microscope. But the fact remained that so far Susan had appeared on *Britain's Got Talent* only once, and that she had a far better chance of establishing a long-term career if she stayed with Simon Cowell, a man who knows the music business inside out. Susan knew that, too, and stuck with it, while expectation built ever higher and the entire world began to dream her dream.

Cowell himself was extremely unamused by Gerry's suggestions, and understandably so. There had been unconfirmed reports that the *Britain's Got Talent* team were worried about Susan's makeover, believing that much of her appeal lay in the contrast between her appearance and her voice, and Gerry's suggestions that she should leave the show prompted an outburst in reply.

'Get yourself together, sweetheart, for the big one — the semi-final,' Cowell advised. 'Shut the door, choose the right song and come back as who you are, not who you want to be.'

It was blunt, certainly, but it was also probably the best advice on offer. But could Susan do it? Could she prove that there was more to her than one performance, however remarkable that had been?

THE HEAT IS ON

Simon Cowell was in trouble again. Not with Gerry Boyle, although Gerry continued to let it be known that he thought his sister should be receiving different treatment, but with little Hollie Steel, the young girl being talked up as one of Susan's main rivals. Simon had publicly poked fun at her tutu, and criticized her choice of number — something that was becoming a stock in trade — but Hollie wasn't having any of it.

'Simon is a bully,' she declared. 'He was very mean to me. He might have thought it was funny, but it's lonely up there on that stage on your own. I'm only ten, and when he said those things about my tutu I felt like I wanted to cry. I had tears in my eyes, but I didn't want him to see me cry like the bullies at school, so I thought of things that made me happy. I thought of being in the final of *Britain's Got Talent* and winning it.' And winning was what she fully intended to do: 'I like Susan but I think I can win this,' declared Hollie. 'I think she is a good singer, but I think I could do better.' With that there was more information about the bullying Hollie had endured at school, and how her parents had scrimped and saved to get her into a good school.

Simon wisely decided not to engage in a war of words with a ten-year-old child, but the banter — if that's what it can be called — and the criticism and the detail about the *BGT* contestants' difficult circumstances were what made the show. The wider audience was engaging not just with the performance on the television, but with the life and times of the contestants, and the more problems they'd had, the more likely the public were to empathize. No one loves the underdog as much as the British, and with each tear-strewn tale came a wave of sympathy and a rise in viewing figures. Cowell the master manipulator knew this as well as anyone, and he also knew that being criticized in the press by *BGT* performers made for very good publicity. Everyone was happy; they were all getting what they wanted now.

Cowell also knew that it made good copy when he had a go at the contestants, so poor Susan got another tongue lashing from him.

By now the Obamas had invited her to sing at the White House, while The Simpsons wanted her to warble to them, prompting Simon to snarl that he was 'fed up' with all the attention she was getting.

'She's not a winner yet,' he commented. 'She's got four weeks to prepare for the biggest night of her life and she's got to sing better than she sang before. But it could all go horribly wrong for her because there are so many other distractions.' He did, however, have the grace to add that he was embarrassed by the judges' initial reaction to Susan: 'We were all guilty on the panel of judging her before she sang, and we all got it utterly wrong,' he admitted. 'You watch it back and it's embarrassing.'

Someone else who had got Susan wrong was Michael Barrymore. As the excitement continued to mount, footage emerged from an episode of Barrymore's 1995 show, *My Kind of People.* Susan had been on it and sang to the great man; he in return totally failed to notice what was in front of him, made a few jokes at her expense — including trying to look up her skirt — and sent her off with a peck on the cheek. The footage had never been televised, and only emerged because Elizabeth MacLean had also been auditioning and was being filmed by her daughter, Julie Febers.

'Susan was a few people in front of me,' Elizabeth told the *Mirror*. 'When she began to sing, I knew she had a great voice, but Michael Barrymore was taking the mickey out of her. This was mine and Susan's second audition for *My Kind of People*. When I saw her on *Britain's Got Talent*, I couldn't believe it was the same Susan . . . I was gobsmacked and I had my hand up to my mouth.'

Barrymore's loss was Simon Cowell's gain. Not that Susan was too worried about that: she had gone into hiding again, after the war of words intensified between her brothers and Cowell. Gerard had already had his say; now it was John's turn, and his view was much the same as his brother's.

'Just let her sing,' he said. 'We're pleading with Simon Cowell to loosen the reins. The hype and celebrity don't mean anything to Susan — she just wants to sing. It is all she has ever wanted to do. Finally she has the chance to show the whole world her amazing talent, but she isn't being allowed to. The whole world is crying out to hear Susan sing again — they want a product, be it an album or a single — but they want it now. We are more and more worried about her health. She is not used to all this and when

I speak to her she sounds exhausted. When Susan signed a contract tying her to *Britain's Got Talent* before her audition, no one could have predicted what a phenomenon she would become. The normal rules don't apply any more — and I think Simon Cowell knows it, too. This is a unique situation and needs a unique solution.'

Both brothers clearly had their sister's wellbeing at heart, and it must have been extremely frustrating for Susan not to be able to show the world what she could do. But a public spat between her family and her mentor was most certainly not going to do her any favours.

It didn't help that Piers Morgan had now stepped into the row, appearing to play down the depth of Susan's talent at a press conference in California. The worry was that Susan would become too big for her boots, but what no one seemed to realize was that, far from becoming big-headed, she was finding it increasingly difficult to cope. While her brothers might have been able to trade blows with Cowell and Morgan, Susan was not. What she needed was for all of them to shield and protect her, not start behaving like stags clashing antlers. None of this was in her best interests and it wasn't surprising that she felt increasingly stressed.

At least Ant and Dec were being supportive, although even they expressed doubts about Susan's changing appearance. 'I don't know about her makeover — she wants to look and feel good and that's her prerogative,' said Dec. 'But she doesn't have to do it 'cos the whole world fell in love with Susan as she was. I can't wait to see her again. I can't wait to see how she is feeling and to see what more she can do. We have only heard the one song from her and I want to hear more.'

'We knew there were some crackers in the auditions,' added Ant. 'Susan is the favourite, but as the weeks go on you can see there's more talent out there. It is not a one-horse race.'

What the other talent didn't have, however, was Susan's international appeal. Over in the States, where Piers and Simon were doing their bit, fascination for Susan continued to grow. Ryan Seacrest, the host of *American Idol* — another of Simon's many projects — revealed that a follower on Twitter had asked when Susan would be a guest on the show, which he called a 'genius idea'. The chances of it happening right then, of course, were pretty low given that Simon wanted Susan to concentrate on *Britain's*

Got Talent, but it was an indication of the level of interest in America — interest that would only grow.

All this interest provoked a rash of stories suggesting that Susan was on the verge of quitting *Britain's Got Talent.* In actual fact nothing could have been further from the truth. The show had given her the most fantastic opportunity, and she wasn't going to blow it now, even if she did have to wait weeks before she could sing again. People might have made comments about Susan's mental ability, but she was canny enough to know that to walk away at this stage would have been madness. And the fact that this wasn't the first time she had sought a big break into television meant that she knew how rare these opportunities were. She wasn't going to throw it away.

Soon problems of a different nature reared their head when it turned out that some of the other acts were thinking of walking on the grounds that Susan winning seemed to be a foregone conclusion. The saxophone player Julian Smith even came out and said as much: 'I don't think I can compete with Susan,' he complained. 'I feel no one else has a chance. She's captured the world's imagination.' Other acts were said to feel the same way, and it was certainly true that none of the other acts had found a way into the public's hearts in quite the same way, but that didn't actually mean Susan was guaranteed to win.

Again the world piled in with their opinions. Piers wrote on his blog, 'I think Hollie can beat Susan. And so can Shaheen from last week. So can a few other acts you haven't seen yet.' The intention was clear: to show the world that there was everything left for everyone to play for, not that that helped Susan. Even her great supporter Demi Moore voiced concern: 'Just seen Hollie,' she tweeted. 'Wow, the talent keeps on coming. More competition for Susan.' On a more positive note, however, it was reported that Catherine Zeta-Jones was interested in playing Susan in a film of her life. Hollywood had certainly lost none of its fascination with what was going on across the pond.

As tempers frayed, expectations soared and controversy mounted, Susan inadvertently caused another row by seeming to imply that her appearance on the show hadn't been the extraordinary chance everyone had thought, but was a result of the show being fixed. She was asked on an American television channel, 'Did the show

91

find you or did you find the show,' to which Susan replied, 'No, the show found me.' This sparked a furore on the internet, with claims that *Britain's Got Talent*'s producers knew exactly what they were doing when they picked out this wee Scottish lady. After all, she had auditioned for Barrymore! The claims were hotly disputed by the show's producers: 'How exactly would we find Susan?' demanded one member of the production staff. 'She's not exactly someone who sticks out from the crowd. For years she has been looking after her mum and living an ordinary life. In no way did the producers hand pick her for the show.'

Indeed, it appeared that in reality what Susan meant was that she had been trying to find somewhere to show off her talent and, having seen Paul Potts on *Britain's Got Talent* the previous year, decided that this was the place to do it. To date there have certainly been no serious allegations that she was hand picked in advance, but at the time it added to the rumours and clamour surrounding the show. Not that anyone involved could really have minded — it was becoming one of the most talked-about shows of the decade.

It did seem incredible, though, that it had taken so long for Susan's talent to be recognized, especially when another video surfaced from 1984. This one was truly jaw-dropping in the light of what the world knew about Susan. It was taken at Mother-well FC's Fir Park Social Club, which was staging a singing contest between the locals and Coventry's Tam O'Shanter Club, and Susan was seconded in to sing when someone dropped out. She performed 'I Don't Know How To Love Him' and 'Memories', the theme tune from *The Way We Were,* and her voice is as clear, strong and powerful as it is today. But what really knocks the viewer for six is Susan's appearance.

The video of Susan singing so many years ago established beyond a shadow of a doubt that Susan was an extremely pretty young woman. This isn't just a polite compliment to a lady coping with a great deal of un-favourable comment about her appearance in middle age; it's a fact. Susan was slim, had prominent cheekbones, clear skin and a mass of dark, curly hair. She sang with confidence and grace, and anyone viewing the video would have considered her quite a catch.

Her appearance in middle age showed, it seemed, how life had taken its toll. She had led a pretty selfless existence, spending almost her entire adult life doing charity work and looking after her mother, but seeing the video of a young Susan dispels any surprise about the fact that she scrubbed up well. The only surprise is that Susan didn't attract more admirers in her youth, although when she left the stage, she is quite clearly seen receiving a kiss. Had she still looked like that when she appeared on *Britain's Got Talent,* she would never have been on the receiving end of the comments she had to endure.

Gerry McGuinness, a school caretaker who took the video, and unearthed it twenty-five years later, certainly thought so. 'I can remember that she was a shy young girl, but also very attractive back then — she turned a few heads when she came into the club,' he told the *Daily Record,* which also put the clip on its website. 'She was not even supposed to be singing, but agreed to perform for the Tam O'Shanter team because someone had dropped out. Even back then I don't think anyone expected too much from her because she was so shy, but when she began singing people took notice. I watched Susan on *Britain's Got Talent* but didn't recognize her as the girl from my video until a relation called and asked if I still had the tape.'

The answer was that he did. 'When I realized who it was, I called my son Jamie in Wishaw and told him I was sending up the video,' Gerry continued. 'It's great Susan is finally getting some recognition. She is a great singer and it seems right that at some point she would get the credit she deserved.'

Jamie was also pretty staggered. 'It is just amazing that nobody realized what a talent she was until now,' he said. 'When you watch the video, it seems so obvious that she was born to be a star.'

The video was, in some ways, just a forerunner of Susan's extraordinary performance two and a half decades later. Everyone who had known her as a young girl talked constantly about her shyness, which had clearly been a burden she had been forced to overcome. But watching her perform all those years ago, the shyness is not apparent. There's something slightly modest about the way she looks as she sings, but she's able to put body and soul into the song and immerse herself in it entirely. As she herself said after she became famous, when she sang, she was able to communicate with the world in a way she couldn't through speech. And just as in 'I Dreamed A Dream', she really inhabited the song 'Memories' and made it her own, another quality that made her stand out from the rest. The song is about a woman looking back over a past love affair — something it was well known that Susan had never experienced — and yet she sang the song with real emotion and pathos. It could have been her own memories she was looking back on that night, and a love that had once burned brightly but was now lost.

Her previous shyness only served to highlight how far Susan had come. If it was still there — and it was — she was hiding it well: for all the strain of being under constant surveillance, there were still plenty of cheery waves to photographers, journalists, passers-by and well-wishers. Perhaps twenty-five years previously Susan had hoped that someone would see her performance at Motherwell FC's Fir Park Social Club and make her a star: she'd certainly had to wait a long time to be recognized since then. Nor was the wait over, for Susan had still not been allowed to sing publicly since her first audition, and many surrounding her feared that if she wasn't allowed to do something soon she'd miss her chance.

Susan proved more patient and sensible, though, biding her time, and eventually Cowell relented and gave an interview in which he admitted how extraordinary the SuBo phenomenon was: 'It's early days, but

Susan could become the biggest star I've ever discovered,' he told the *Daily Record*. 'She's got a real shot this year of doing something phenomenal for herself, probably more than she realizes. I think every record label in the world would want to sign Susan right now. She is in a fantastic position.' She just had to be patient.

Cowell had been in the music business for a long time, but even he was taken aback by the scale of Susan's popularity. 'I have never seen anything like it in my life,' he said. 'Susan is the biggest entertainment story this year. It has dominated the news for weeks and never gone off the radar. It's the biggest phenomenon I've ever seen out of any of my shows. I've never seen anything travel so quickly, particularly what happened on the internet. She's got the world at her feet right now — but there's no need to panic. I read about her family saying they want to capitalize on this, and right now I think that would be a huge mistake. The offers she is getting from people won't go away. There's going to be as much support for Susan in one year's time or two years' time. I had a very similar situation with Paul Potts, where people were asking should he capitalize on his fame, but I said, "No, this is just part of the process." He went on with the rest of the competition, he was treated fairly, he won and sold five million records.'

It was sound advice from a man who had been there, done that and got the T-shirt. Simon was able to keep an eye on the bigger picture, so much so that he could envisage a future that even Susan couldn't imagine for herself.

'Susan is representing Scotland in a huge talent competition,' he said. 'Dropping out would be like Scotland being in the World Cup and saying just before the final, "You know what? I don't think we'll enter." Broadway and Hollywood are possibilities for Susan, but it's one step at a time at the moment. We have to take it a week at a time, and if she achieves what I think she can, then it's going to be an incredible end for her in *Britain's Got Talent.* That opportunity shouldn't be taken away from her now.'

Simon Cowell is not a man known for apologizing, but he did now: 'I would love to sit her down for five minutes and say, "Susan, you proved a point, you turned us around in five seconds, I apologize we ever doubted you," ' he went on. ' "We are supporting you, we want you to do well and we're going to be there for you." The second Susan walked on, I think the audience smelled blood. I think they thought it was probably going to last about five seconds because she looked nervous, she had a funny walk and she was finding it difficult to answer my questions. And there was no doubt we all thought this was probably going to be an audition that lasts about five seconds. Then of course she started singing. I don't think we've ever been shut up so quickly in our lives. The way she affected the audience was astonishing. One minute they were about to boo her, and the next she's got them in the palm of her hand. Right now she is one of the most famous people in the world. If nothing else happens, she has acceptance and, for whatever reason, I don't think she had that before.'

Cowell was spot on. Susan's music had always been her salvation, and now it was leading her into a whole different world of opportunity. The young Susan on the video, with so much to look forward to, had lived a difficult life, but her talent had endured, and now it was bringing her acceptance. Whatever life had in store for her, she would always have that astonishing audition and the respect she'd garnered that day.

In the meantime, *Britain's Got Talent* continued to motor on. Cowell has a genius for publicity — something no one can doubt —

and when a promising contestant didn't have a suitable back story, he managed to pull one out of a hat by creating an on-air feud.

The latest contestant to get through to the semi-final was Sue Son, a violinist from London, but for Sue, things hadn't quite gone according to plan. She'd come on the show as one half of a classical duo called Addicted, with her friend Janine Khalil. In a stroke of Mephistophelean brilliance, Simon suggested that Sue split from Janine and strike out on her own, which Sue, of course, did. Jealousy and accusations of betrayal followed — and all on national television. Initially Janine said that she would have done the same, but then she appeared to change her mind.

'I thought everything was fine,' said Sue somewhat naively. 'Later she admitted she was devastated. She didn't want me to do the show. I thought she would be a true friend and support me but she's been ignoring my calls and has blocked me on Facebook. She even called my mum the other day in Korea at 3 a.m., telling her I'd betrayed her. I can't believe she would do that — contacting my mum at three in the morning talking about how I'd betrayed her. It's awful.' But it certainly made good TV.

Meanwhile it was suggested that Susan should become the face of a cosmetics company — she'd certainly made a dramatic change in her appearance — or make an appearance on *I'm A Celebrity . . . Get Me Out Of Here!,* also presented by Ant and Dec. In truth, for a woman like Susan, there could hardly have been a less suitable show, but no one seemed to have realized that yet.

The next contestant to get through was Jamie Pugh. He had a very sad story to tell as his wife had died of cancer ten years earlier. But to his great credit he didn't make a song and dance about it, confining himself to talking about his nerves instead.

Someone else who was taking a keen interest in the show was one of the very few people who might have understood how Susan was feeling — Paul Potts — although even he hadn't come under such intensive scrutiny. As the very first winner of *Britain's Got Talent,* Potts was a similarly unlikely artist, with an equally unconventional appearance, although because he was a man it seemed to matter less and cause less comment in the media. Nor did he have to put up with the male equivalent of the 'virgin spinster' tag that had been firmly attached to Susan. He had, however, been thrown from a life of quiet obscurity into the media limelight, and more to the point, he had built a lasting career on the back of it.

Potts was quick to offer Susan his support: 'I think she's great, I think she's in with a great chance,' he said. 'But there are a number of people who also stand a chance and I'm conscious of the fact that the set-up is slightly different this year. She did week one and has got a lot more pressure on her. I wish her well. I think she's done really well and she's coped with the media attention. I don't know how I would have coped with suddenly finding photographers on my doorstep.' He was also conscious of the commercial possibilities of working together: 'I'd be looking at a duet in the future,' he continued. 'But it's early days yet. I wouldn't want to add any more pressure than she has already. She's taking every new day as it comes. She has to enjoy it as much as possible and not think about the pressure of her next performance, because that will be different.'

In truth, Susan was thinking of little else apart from her next performance. She had been spotted with a list of songs by Andrew Lloyd Webber in her hand, leading to intense speculation about what she would perform next, a crucial decision if she were to prove she wasn't a one-trick pony. All this time the stage of *Britain's Got Talent* was filling up with children, and one night in mid-May there were no fewer than six acts on stage featuring youngsters. They had the benefit of the cuteness factor, and Amanda energetically leaping to her feet to applaud as often as she could, but despite this, none of them created as memorable a moment as Susan had.

The semi-final was drawing near now, putting Susan under even greater pressure, and although there were to be some much publicized quivers, Susan was showing every sign of being able to square up to her new life.

The measure of her celebrity became clear when she was invited to appear on the queen of all chat shows, *The Oprah Winfrey Show.* Susan's neighbours in Blackburn had become accustomed to seeing television crews camped on her lawn, but this was the big one. The team from *Oprah* duly arrived and set up *chez* Susan, where she started off by giving them a tour of her house — an extremely modest affair in global celebrity standards.

In many ways it was a clever move, for Susan had had little direct contact with the public since becoming an overnight star, and while her appearance on *Oprah* didn't allow her to sing, it did mean she could comment on all the stories that had been flying around.

Her appearance had required permission from the *Britain's Got Talent* team, however, and they had specified that Team Oprah must visit Susan rather than Susan flying to them, since they did not want it to look as though Susan was receiving special treatment. Her appearance did go some way towards deflecting criticism that they were allowing Susan to remain in limbo for so long — a globally recognized singer who wasn't allowed to sing.

The first issue Oprah tackled was the makeover nonsense, which had attracted such criticism from some quarters, as if a woman shouldn't be allowed to make the best of what she had. Given the jibes she'd endured after her first appearance, Susan wouldn't be human if she hadn't wanted to smarten up. 'That was just to tidy myself up like any other female would have done,' she explained. 'Depends what you mean by a makeover. I mean, my best friend actually helps me with my make-up. I mean, that's hardly a makeover.'

Sounding friendly and modest, Susan explained that she was by no means certain she'd win the competition, and that she wasn't lonely at all, given that she had millions of new friends. As for her newfound fame, she said, 'I think change is very hard to get used to at first, but [I'm] really enjoying it, really enjoying every second of it. It's like a dream come true.' Given her Scottish accent, Susan was subtitled for the benefit of the American audience, which greeted her appearance rapturously. Although she still hadn't been there, Susan had admirers aplenty over the pond.

Back in Blighty, Susan was getting ready for her next big appearance. The agonizing wait was very nearly over, and the semifinals of *Britain's Got Talent* were on the horizon. The change in the significance of her first and second appearance could not have been more momentous. While the first time round she had everything to play for, now she had everything to lose. And how on earth could she top that first appearance? Would Susan Boyle be able to pull off another electrifying performance?

ALL ALONE
IN THE SPOTLIGHT

The moment Susan and the rest of the world had been waiting for had very nearly arrived. She had made it through to the semi-finals of *Britain's Got Talent* in its very first week, and now they were about to take place. The tension was mounting and the weight of expectation on Susan was very heavy indeed.

Piers Morgan couldn't resist shoving his oar in, in the run-up to the big day. 'After Susan auditioned for the show and said she'd never been kissed and never had a boyfriend, I did say that I would break her "kissing duck",' he said. 'That offer still stands. I have not seen her since the auditions. So when we meet again, if Susan asks for a kiss, I'll do it . . . on TV.'

Of course it would be on TV — where else? In the event, Susan was wise enough to decline his offer, but Piers had a serious point to make, as well. 'Susan's popularity is a double-edged sword,' he continued. 'If her fans think her winning the show is a foregone conclusion, they may not vote for her. Secondly, Susan must be under more pressure than anyone else. Some 200 million people have seen her sing "I Dreamed A Dream". How can you top that?'

How indeed? The answer is you couldn't, but that didn't necessarily matter. What mattered was that Susan put in an absolutely top-class performance, and to make matters more stressful, this time it was going to be live.

Susan was the first to admit she was feeling the strain: 'The largest audience I have performed to before this show was around 500 people in a local theatre for the Voluntary Arts Council in West Lothian,' she told the *Daily Star.* 'I never even thought I'd get past the judges. I can't believe I am in the semi-finals and I've been overwhelmed by the public reaction to my performance. I will be very nervous but I am just going to go out there and do my best.'

The exact nature of the performance, including what Susan was going to wear and what she would sing, were still a closely guarded secret. Everyone knew how much was at stake, and everyone realized that Susan's was the most eagerly anticipated appearance on the show.

'She has a God-given incredible raw talent and a passion that is second to none,' said Yvie Burnett, the *Britain's Got Talent* voice coach, who had worked with many a big star in the past. 'I have worked with hugely gifted artists, but when it comes to Susan's genre of music, she is the best I have ever had the pleasure of coaching. She will have the whole nation in tears in the live semi-finals. I'll be crying too.'

At least one hoped so, for nothing was set in stone yet. All the judges were quick to say that it wasn't a given that Susan would get through to the final, and at times they seemed impatient about the fuss everyone was making. There were other contestants too, after all — in some cases very good ones — and there was a fear that Susan's rise to prominence had been so sudden she risked a backlash, although in truth there had been no sign of such a thing.

Yvie put her finger on the many qualities that Susan displayed that had made her so popular. 'There is a realness and charm about Susan that you can't help but love,' she said. 'She's a normal woman from a wee village in Scotland who happens to have a stunning voice. I was in America when the show first aired. I was watching the news and the presenter started talking about someone on *British Idol.* I watched in awe as they played her singing "I Dreamed A Dream". No matter whether she wins or not, I can't see her jumping into a limo or living a celebrity lifestyle. She was having a right laugh about her mention on *The Simpsons,* and I think it's her fantastic sense of humour that will help carry her through all the hype.'

She certainly needed something, because the hype was only getting bigger, and at long last, on 24 May, Susan became one of eight acts — there were forty in total — to appear on the first night of the semi-finals. There had been growing reports about backstage nerves, but her performance that night was an utter and absolute triumph.

When the show began, there were clips of Susan's triumphant audition, interspersed with interviews with Susan and some of the leading players in the drama. Susan was pictured looking dreamily out across the Scottish countryside, and what she had to say about herself was in many ways heartbreaking.

'All my life I've had to prove myself, that I can be accepted and that I'm not the worthless person people think I am, that I do have something to offer,' she said, and there was certainly proof of that now. Quite what this meant to her and how much she'd wanted this opportunity — and why — was only too apparent. Many people had thought she had nothing to contribute, but she did, and it wasn't just her magnificent voice either. Susan's kindness and modesty could not have been more apparent: this was a woman who had spent her life in the service of others, and she had a lot to give, all right.

Next Amanda came on. 'This one little woman, from a tiny village in Scotland, has got the whole world talking about her,' she said, and to prove it, news clips were shown from all around the world, lauding Susan. 'I don't think she's really got a clue as to the impact she's made,' said Cowell.

Then there was the question of the internet sensation she'd caused, something that was as big a shock to Susan as anyone else. Indeed, she hadn't really known anything about it, still less how it could play a part in creating a global sensation.

'YouTube was pretty new to me,' said Susan. 'The only tube I knew was a tube of Smarties.' From such a sheltered background as hers, should this be any surprise?

Susan's mentors knew exactly what was at stake, though. 'The whole world is watching

Susan Boyle perform tonight,' said Simon. 'I wouldn't want to be standing where she is right now.'

The screen flashed back to Susan. '*Britain's Got Talent* is the chance to turn things around, to fulfill the dream,' she said. 'I just want that chance to perform in front of the Queen.'

At last it was time for her to take the stage. The scene switched to the auditorium, the three judges, the empty stage and the ebullient hosts, Ant and Dec, who were enjoying themselves as much as ever.

'Here she is!' cried Dec. 'Please welcome . . . Susan Boyle!'

The mirrored doors at the back of the stage opened and out she came, almost unrecognizable from the Susan Boyle we'd met only six weeks earlier. Here was a middle-aged version of the pretty young girl who had sung 'The Way We Were' twenty-five years ago. Her hair had been set in a pleasingly curly style and she was wearing a bronze dress made especially for her. Her face was fully made up, unlike the last time, when she hadn't worn a spot of make-up. This Susan Boyle was a world-famous performer. Now she just had to give the performance of a lifetime.

Susan looked quite calm as she walked

down to the edge of the stage, smiling broadly at the cheering crowd. The music began to swell in the background and it was indeed a song by Andrew Lloyd Webber, the deeply affecting 'Memory', which was taken to be a tribute to Susan's moggy Pebbles since it was from the musical *Cats*.

When Susan began to sing, it seemed as though disaster had struck: she'd started off on the wrong note. Almost immediately, though, she corrected herself, her voice rising and growing stronger than ever above the wildly cheering crowd. She smiled at the audience as she sang, and during the pause in the middle of the song, before resuming again with an exceptionally powerful 'Touch me . . .' By now the audience was hollering and Simon, Amanda and Piers were on their feet. Susan had pulled it off.

Of course there was no longer the shock value of a slightly unkempt woman being revealed to have a beautiful voice, but there was also no doubt about her talent. That first performance had not been a one-off. Susan really was a major new talent who, if handled properly, could have a huge career ahead of her. This time there was no awkward attempt to shuffle off stage as soon as she was done; instead, Ant and Dec bounded up to her, telling her to get her breath back and relax. There was a brief interlude as they told viewers which number to call to vote Susan through to the final, before they got on with the bit everyone wanted to hear.

'Susan, you've been waiting all day to do this,' Dec began. 'How does it feel?'

'Fantastic,' declared Susan emphatically. 'Absolutely fantastic!'

'Good girl!' cried the boys. 'Susan,' continued Ant, 'try to describe what the last few weeks have been like. One hundred million hits on YouTube, you're in the papers, America — how's it been?'

'Unbelievable. Absolutely unbelievable,' Susan replied.

'Did it add to the pressure for tonight, though?' asked Ant.

'What pressure?' asked Susan. 'It was really good tonight. I really enjoyed myself tonight.'

This got a few more cries of 'good girl', before Dec asked if Susan had enjoyed every minute.

'I've enjoyed every second,' she said. 'And I'd do it again.' This elicited more cheers and whoops from the audience, but Susan could have read them the telephone book at that point and they'd have lapped it up. They loved her, and so did the world.

Next it was over to the judges.

'Susan,' Piers began. 'I think you look absolutely beautiful tonight.'

'Thank you very much,' interjected Susan, blowing him a kiss.

'And more importantly, I thought you sang beautifully as well. And the great thing about you, that we've all realized, was that when the world was going through a pretty tough time and was looking for a bit of hope and inspiration, along came Susan Boyle to provide it. And on behalf of the whole world, because they're all watching you tonight, thank you, Susan.' This elicited a roar of enthusiasm from the audience, applause and a storm of cheers. Susan beamed and bowed gracefully in return.

Now it was over to Amanda. 'Susan,' she began, 'you're turning into Eva Peron, it's fantastic. And I am just so relieved that it went so fantastically well for you. I was biting all my acrylic nails off. You nailed that performance. I'm so proud of you and I'm proud that you represented Britain so brilliantly. Because Piers is right and the world is watching you. So well done and thank you.'

Susan thanked her in reply.

Simon began. 'Well, Susie [sic], you are one special lady, I have to say,' he said. 'You really are. And you know what? I just want to apologize because of the way we treated you before you sang the first time. You've made me and everyone else look very stupid and I'm very happy for you and very proud of you.'

Susan lifted her eyebrows and shrugged, saying, 'I know nothing,' a few times. She had taken everything the judges and the world at large had thrown at her like a remarkably good sport.

Dec took over again. 'Thank you very much indeed, judges,' he said. 'Susan, great comments. You must be over the moon.'

Susan nodded emphatically. 'I'm very happy to be here. And thank you all for your support,' she said, and with that she walked off, waving to the enthusiastic crowd.

Susan went through to the next round along with dance troupe Diversity. They had tied with Natalie Okri, so Simon had to use his casting vote, much to the chagrin of the audience. The other acts that weren't successful that night were the violinist Sue Son; Darth Vader/Michael Jackson impersonator Darth Jackson; belly dancer Julia Naidenko; comedy dancing duo Faces of Disco; and street performer Nick Hell.

Once again, though, it had been Susan's night.

The papers were full of praise the next day, with headlines such as 'Sue Perb!' and 'Sue Perstar'. Simon Cowell was now talking seriously about making a film of her life and, whether she won *Britain's Got Talent* or not, there was almost certainly going to be a CD. Nearly 14 million viewers had tuned in to see the show and the biggest draw, without a doubt, had been Susan.

Susan herself was feeling fine, larking about and enjoying herself. In the aftermath of the show, she bumped into Piers and finally got that kiss: 'I've been kissed now,' she said impishly before laughing and running away.

'It was very exciting,' said a gallant Piers. 'I felt very proud to be the man who did it, as I thought she looked absolutely beautiful on Sunday.'

And as for that initial bum note, there turned out to be a reason for it: Susan had been struggling with a cold. 'It was a pretty rocky start to begin with because I sort of hit a croaky note,' she explained afterwards. 'That's because I had a cold, but I said to myself, "I guess you'd better just pick yourself up and keep going," so all I did was keep going after that and it got better.'

Now there was the final to look forward to.

'I'm really looking forward to the final and to giving an improved act,' Susan continued. 'I really want to fulfill this dream and see it through to the end. I'm feeling really good. The audience reaction was really stunning and it feels really good to have fans all around the world. It's overwhelming. It's very hard to put into words.'

As the semi-finals went on, the next two to get through were Flawless and Shaun Smith, both of whom wowed the judges.

'Earlier tonight on the TV news I said if Susan Boyle doesn't win this contest I am a doughnut,' said Piers. 'I may have to consider the prospect of being a doughnut.'

They were then followed by the Greek dance duo Stavros Flatley and Shaheen Jafargholi.

Behind the scenes, there were indications that the strain was beginning to show on Susan. At this stage, the full extent of her learning difficulties hadn't been made clear, so the public was startled by the erratic behaviour she suddenly began to display.

When she appeared on *Britain's Got More Talent,* her answers to the questions put to her seemed disjointed and a little eccentric. When she was asked what she thought of a doll that was based on her, instead of answering, she put it beside her nose. Then there was an unfortunate incident at the Wembley Plaza hotel, where all the contestants were staying. A group of them were watching the semi-finals when Piers announced that Shaheen was producing 'pound for pound the best singing performance in the semi-finals.' This was the very same Piers who Susan had admitted having a crush on and who had just boasted about giving Susan her first proper kiss. Susan appeared singularly unable to cope, and allegedly, according to onlookers (although Susan was to deny the incident took place), she gave the TV screen a two-fingered salute and shouted, 'Fuck off,' before walking out.

This was neither the language nor the behaviour the country expected of the prim and proper spinster, but it soon emerged that this was the way she used to react when confronted with the irritating juveniles who used to taunt her at home. It was a bit of a jolt to the national consciousness, not least because it was the first time the public realized that Susan's problems might run a little deeper than simply never having been kissed and living alone.

It was also the first time Susan had experienced a celebrity 'downer'. Although at times it seemed as though half of Hollywood's A list were publicly backing her, there was the odd dissenting voice, such as Lily Allen's when she tweeted that Susan was 'overrated'.

'I thought her timing was off on Sunday — no control, and I don't think she has an amazing voice,' Allen continued. 'She can sing, but it's not about talent with her, is it?'

This provoked an immediate row. The Secretary of State for Scotland, Jim Murphy, felt moved to criticize Lily, telling her he couldn't have agreed less, while Ladbrokes announced that it expected Susan to garner more Number Ones than Lily.

Suddenly everything had stopped running as smoothly as it had been, and there were more problems to come. Craig Revel Horwood, a judge on *Strictly Come Dancing*, waded into the debate by saying that Susan was a 'freak of nature'. The media printed a picture of Susan arguing with two policemen, who had been called after she rounded on a reporter who had asked her about the incident where she'd shouted at the TV.

Although she had denied the earlier incident, more and more negative comments about her were appearing and fears were growing that her fragile mental state might stop her taking part in the show's final. This would be a disaster for everyone: the producers of the show, who would lose their biggest draw, and for Susan herself, who had the opportunity of a lifetime within her grasp. Something had to be done, and fast. Behind the scenes there were urgent consultations about her mental state, while Piers made a very public plea on his blog for Susan's critics to back off.

'Imagine, if you will, being anonymous for forty-seven years of your life, and then suddenly being propelled into genuine world superstardom,' he wrote. 'For many people, it would be a dream come true. All that fame and attention and the prospect of all that money to come with it down the line. The pressure from sudden global success can be enormous. Imagine having all this going on when you are days away from the final of a competition that can make or break your career and your life. A competition that everyone expects you to win, a fact that in itself piles on even more pressure. This is exactly the situation that Susan Boyle now finds herself in. And my heart absolutely bleeds for the poor woman.

'She was said to be angry because I, her

"favourite judge", had backed another contestant. Susan denies this happened and I wasn't there, so I don't know what really went on. But I've seen the photos of her arguing with policemen and I've read the incredibly bitchy comments exploding all over various websites. And you know what? It made me very, very angry. Susan Boyle is a very kind, generous-hearted lady who has had a pretty tough life. I am calling for everyone to just give her a break.'

Piers was doing his utmost to help Susan at this low point by spending time with her, trying to calm her down and telling the public to back off. Susan had been, he said, on the verge of walking out on the show because the pressure was so intense, and she was becoming increasingly distressed by the negative comments that were beginning to flow. She had been in tears, according to Piers, and was like a 'rabbit in the headlights'. What poor Susan was experiencing, of course, was tall poppy syndrome — the British urge to cut anyone down to size who appears to stand out from the rest. Just about every famous Briton has had to endure it at one stage or another — including Simon, Piers and Amanda, all of whom had received drubbings from the press and public over the years — but unlike them,

Susan was ill-equipped to cope.

'I am today calling for everyone to just give Susan a break,' Piers blogged. 'She is two days away from the biggest day of her life, and all she wants to do is sing well for everyone and hopefully try to win . . . She was deprived of oxygen during her birth, and that left her with learning difficulties, causing her to be called 'Simple Susan' at school. She's only been able to have one brief job in her life, but rather than feel sorry for herself she dedicated all her time to helping her ageing, ailing mother until she died two years ago. Susan's just a sweet, middle-aged lady from a Scottish village, who can't really comprehend the sheer scale of what's happened to her.'

Did it help? At least Piers managed to persuade Susan to stay on the show, but it was the start of a troubling period for Susan, who, having coped so well until now, seemed to be succumbing to the strain of it all. It was as if the stresses of the previous few weeks had suddenly overwhelmed her, and if that were not enough, there were family worries, too. One of her nieces, who had just given birth, had a fall shortly afterwards, brought on by a dizzy spell.

Not for the first time since the circus began, Susan was spirited out of public view in order to relax and wind down. The first time she had hidden away because she couldn't cope with the sudden popularity, but this time the opposite was the case. That said, however, it was only a tiny minority who gave her stick. She still had a huge global fan base — a few silly incidents weren't going to stop that — and on the whole, the world was behind her as much as ever. She was still their Cinderella and they wanted to see her go to the ball.

The problem is that nastiness is louder than moral support, so all Susan heard were the negative comments. She didn't realize that for every naysayer, there were a hundred well-wishers, and why should she? This was a woman who had been bullied her entire life, so it must have seemed as though things were returning to the way they'd always been.

The other judges were equally concerned. *Britain's Got Talent* was Simon's show, and he wanted to ensure her wellbeing, so he met up with her and told her not to give up on her dream by walking out. 'I wanted to make sure she is OK,' he told reporters afterwards. 'I wanted to tell her I would help her in any way I can. She has earned the right to be in that final and I didn't want her to miss out on her big night.'

'Susan's not going to quit,' Amanda confirmed. 'I think she did have her bags packed at one stage, but I think basically that was just because she was feeling so sad and kind of upset. We've just got to keep being on her side and not assume she's going to win. [But] I would imagine that whether she wins or loses, she will definitely record "I Dreamed A Dream". I think that that would be a huge, huge hit. It would go platinum.'

By the time the final rolled round the negative comments had died down — in the press at least — as commentators began to realize that while picking on Susan made good copy, it was actually doing her harm. But there was now another worry for the show's organizers: what would happen if Susan *didn't* win. It didn't matter as far as viewing figures, the subsequent tour or anything else was concerned; what did worry them was how Susan would react. There was increasing public criticism of the show for putting a vulnerable lady in the spotlight, so if Susan lost and went into meltdown, how would that make them look?

Sensing that this problem should be tackled before it got blown out of all proportion, Piers once more spoke up. As an ex-newspaper editor and seasoned media figure, he had the hide of a rhinoceros and nerves of steel, but he could see vulnerability when it appeared in front of him, and he wanted to protect Susan as much as he could. Susan had publicly named him as the man she had a crush on, so perhaps that made him feel even more responsible for her. By this time Piers appeared to be Susan's unofficial protector, and if the outcome everyone was expecting didn't happen, then he would be responsible for heading off any negative reactions.

'Susan's going to be a major star, whatever happens,' he said. 'And I for one hope she absolutely nails it on the night and shoves all these vile critics' disgraceful attacks down their throats. Will she win? In many ways, Susan Boyle's already won. As for all the furore surrounding Susan, my bet is that she will respond with the performance of her life at the final. This is one tough lady who has had to fight since the day she was born. And there is no way she's going to quit now.'

The programme makers were certainly doing what they could to help. Richard Holloway, one of the show's producers, was keen to point out that as well as being subject to the kind of attention more usually associated with the likes of Brad Pitt and Angelina Jolie, Susan was being given constant support. A friend was accompanying her to London, and when she was in Scotland, a member of the show's production staff was always in situ.

Meanwhile, lots of media-friendly psychiatrists were being wheeled out to give their views. Some thought she should go ahead with the contest, some thought she shouldn't, so she didn't have to deal with the trauma of her star fading at some point — it didn't occur to anyone that it might not — and there was general agreement that Susan's perception that Piers had withdrawn his support by praising Shaheen had been very upsetting for her. The lady herself, however, kept shtum.

The pressure was certainly greater than ever before. Back in Blackburn, the locals were preparing a huge celebration, which was to be held whatever the outcome of the competition, while plans were afoot for the town to get together in The Happy Valley Hotel to watch Susan perform on the show. They were totally unfazed by Susan's outbursts, not least because they'd seen them before: 'I've known Susan all her life,' said David Stein, the village butcher. 'We know what Susan can do verbally; she can be pretty rough on you.'

Jackie Russell, the manager of the pub, agreed. 'It's the stress,' she said. 'It's only natural. She's used to just walking up and down to the shops and nobody bothering her, and all of a sudden she's thrust into this limelight. It must be really hard for her.'

One thing was for certain, interest in Susan kept mounting, with speculation about what she would wear and sing increasing by the day. For a woman who had had to put up with a lot of stick about her appearance, she was now in the bizarre position of being treated as something of a fashion icon. She also remained the bookies' favourite to win.

The stage was set for the next big act in Susan's life, but Piers was right: whatever happened she was already a star. If she'd messed up the semi-final — and the speed of her recovery from that duff note was proof that she hadn't — it's unlikely her career would have progressed any further. Instead, however, her appearance had been a triumph, showing that she was no flash in the pan. As painful as it was for her to go through, Susan's problems only increased the public's fascination with her. Clearly, apart from a few strange souls, no one wanted her to suffer; everyone wanted her to thrive. But the fact that her battles weren't entirely over kept the public glued to the soap opera, wondering what was going to happen next. Susan was a star, all right, but she was still going to have to battle on.

A MASSIVE UPSET

The final of *Britain's Got Talent* was finally here — on 30 May 2009 — and tensions were running about as high as they could get. Susan had seemed like a shoe-in at first, but just recently doubts had been raised as to whether she would make it through — not that it mattered much. Susan's musical career looked guaranteed, whatever happened on stage that night. Even so, she wanted to win, and the goodwill towards her remained palpable: the country wanted her to win, too.

The nation's television sets switched on and the contest began. As the show started, they repeated clips of the earlier stages of the proceedings, and another interview with Susan, resplendent in a neat yellow blouse.

'When I first applied to *Britain's Got Talent,* I never really realized I'd be sitting here, in the final,' she said. 'If I win this people will see I'm not the person who's just living at home with just the cat. They'll see a new person, a new Susan Boyle, a Susan Boyle the singer. Through this I can walk down the street and be proud of who I am.'

Piers came up on the screen. 'Susan Boyle has gone from being a totally anonymous spinster from a Scottish village to one of the most famous women on the planet in several weeks,' he said as an array of international papers, all with headlines about Susan, flashed up on the screen. 'That brings with it massive pressure.'

Back to Susan: 'The pressure put on me this week has been overwhelming,' she said. 'But I've got to learn to put that aside.' They were brave words, but it was easier said than done.

Now it was Simon's turn. 'For anybody, this is intense. Huge, huge, huge pressure,' he said. 'And now she's got to sing.'

Back to Susan. 'It's the most important night of my life tonight,' she said. 'When I step on that stage, it will be the accumulation of forty years of dreaming. A life-long ambition.'

And so it was time for the performance. Ant and Dec introduced her and there she was again, dressed in a long, silvery blue gown, singing 'I Dreamed A Dream' once more. Susan's performance was as powerful and assured as before, but her expression was different. There was a more troubled dimension to it than there had been in the past. Susan had had a rotten week enduring a public backlash that had left her feeling vulnerable. For all the brilliance of her performance — and no matter how miserable she might have been feeling, nothing could stifle the beauty of her voice — you could see that all was not well in the world of Susan Boyle.

Despite her troubles, the audience loved it. There were screams and applause, and the three judges all leapt to their feet, cheering and whooping. Susan smiled, though whether it was with relief or genuine enjoyment, it was impossible to tell, then Ant and Dec bounded on stage like frolicsome little puppies, determined to cheer up the diminutive singer with the magnificent voice.

'Well done, Susan,' said Ant. 'Fantastic reaction, all of the judges on their feet. How was that for you? You've had a lot of pressure on you this week, but you went out there and performed and it seemed like you really enjoyed that.'

'I want to thank the people for all the support they've given me,' said Susan, who appeared to be a little more nervous than on previous occasions, 'especially the people at home, the people in the audience — everybody. I'd like to thank you for all your support.'

Her comment was greeted by a round of applause.

'It's been a week full of pressure for all the acts here tonight, none more so than you,' began Dec. 'Was that worth it, in front of everybody here?'

'Well worth it!' cried Susan emphatically.

'That's where you really feel at home, on stage?' asked Dec.

'Of course I do. I'm among friends, am I not?' asked Susan, getting the audience cheering once more.

'Of course you are, and let's go to the judges and find out,' said Ant. 'Piers, what did you think of Susan's performance?'

'Wow,' said Piers. 'Susan, you've had a very difficult week — you've had an amazing seven weeks, but you've had a very difficult week where you've been the centre of the world's attention. There's been negative headlines, you've been "boiling over", "cracking up", going to "quit the show", all this kind of thing, and quietly, what I kept thinking to myself was, All you have to do to answer all your critics is to walk down that stage to that microphone, sing the song that we all fell in love with, sing it better than you did last time — and Susan, I'm not supposed to favour anyone in this competition as a judge, I should be impartial, but you know what? Forget it. That to me was the greatest performance I've seen in *Britain's Got Talent*'s history. You should win this competition. I loved it.'

The audience was cheering again: they clearly agreed. Susan looked gracious up on the stage, and while Piers clearly meant it, it was the least he could say. After all, he had, inadvertently, been responsible for causing some of the distress she'd experienced that week. A very public avowal of loyalty from Piers was exactly what Susan needed at that stage.

Now it was Amanda's turn. 'Susan, I have never heard such powerful, confident vocals,' she began. 'You sang it so well this evening and I just echo what Piers said, really. You, out of everybody this week, have been under an enormous amount of pressure, but you did it, girl. You did it for Scotland and you did it for Great Britain.' There was more thunderous applause. 'And can I just say,' Amanda added, 'Simon had a tear in his eye. And I've never seen that before.'

Finally, it was the turn of the maestro. Brushing aside questions from Ant as to whether Amanda's comment was true, he said, 'I don't know who's going to win this competition, but you know, you've had a weird seven weeks. You had every right to walk away from this, and you could have walked away. You could have had a lot of stuff coming your way in America, and a lot of people said you shouldn't even be in this competition. That you're not equipped to deal with it. For what? For you to sit at home with your cat and say, "I've missed an opportunity." I completely disagree with that. Well, I do. And you know, win or lose, you have the guts to come back here tonight, face your critics and you beat them. And that's the most important thing.'

In the background, the cheers started again.

'Whatever happens, Susan,' Simon continued, 'and you know, I've got to know the real Susan Boyle, which is not the person I've seen portrayed in the media, who is a very nice, shy person who just wants a break, you can walk away from this, win or lose, with your head held high, Susan. I absolutely adore you.'

'That makes me feel really good, thanks very much,' said Susan, blowing a kiss as she left the stage.

■ ■ ■ ■

Back in her hometown of Blackburn, the atmosphere was electric. Over a hundred locals had gathered in the Happy Valley to watch the show, and when Susan walked on stage, total silence descended. Throughout the village, almost everyone was glued to their TV screens, and when her performance ended, the place erupted. Susan was certainly a winner there.

Back in London, though, it was a different story. To everyone's surprise and consternation, Susan didn't win on the night — that honour went to the dance troupe Diversity. Susan remained gracious in defeat though: 'They're very entertaining,' she said. 'The best act won.' But even so it was hard not to feel cheated. This modern-day Cinderella had been at the heart of a fairytale, and the nation expected a fairytale ending. They didn't get one.

Everyone involved was shocked. 'Susan was there at the top all along, but she was incredibly gracious,' said Simon Cowell as the news sunk in. 'She's won a lot of people over and people have got to see the real Susan. She's incredible.'

'Can I just say on behalf of all of us that it

was amazing to meet you,' said Dec. Although he was far too professional to say so, it looked as if he thought they'd got the wrong result, too.

Despite losing the competition, there was no question that it would put a stop to Susan's meteoric rise — matters had gone too far for that — but it did underline some real concerns. Susan had seemed certain to win, and the fact that she hadn't was ascribed in some quarters to the negative publicity she'd received in the run-up to the show. People didn't seem to understand that her erratic behaviour was a direct result of her learning difficulties, and just thought Susan was being temperamental. The majority may not have thought like that, but a vocal minority did, and it had damaged her chances. That was almost certainly the real reason she didn't win.

And that led directly to the next question: with the weight of expectation lying heavy on her shoulders, how was she going to take it now that she'd lost? Was Susan going to go off the rails? As the judges had acknowledged, this had been a nerve-racking week for all the contestants, but especially Susan. There had never been a phenomenon like her before, and no one seemed certain quite what to do next. With the *Britain's Got Tal-*

ent tour coming up, decisions had to be made, and the question on everyone's lips was, would Susan be well enough to attend? She would be the biggest pull on the tour, but if she joined it would the producers be blamed for putting her under even more pressure when she was clearly unable to cope?

Susan herself could be forgiven for not taking it all in. Asked what she'd do next, she replied bravely, 'I hope to get an album out and I'll just play it by ear. What a journey. It was unbelievable and very humbling. Thank you for everything.'

Susan's family and friends were becoming increasingly concerned, but at least she had the support of her friend Lorraine Campbell, who had been at school with Susan, and was staying in London with her, acting as a shoulder to cry on, as well as a much-needed rock. Having known Susan all her life, she was able to calm her down when she got too het up, and she also took Susan to Mass when she was feeling overwhelmed. Even so, it was becoming obvious that ultimately Susan was going to need professional help.

Susan still had a future, though, and a very profitable one at that. Estimates started flying around about how much money

Susan would make out of it all, and while the amounts varied wildly, soaring up to £10 million, there was no doubt that she stood to earn more than the show's £100,000 prize money. Her brother John certainly forecast great things: 'The world will definitely hear from Susan Boyle again,' he said. 'The show is by no means over. Hopefully now she can relax a bit and just sing, which is all she ever wanted to do. The family are delighted and proud. She put on a tremendous show. Our parents will be looking down with big smiles on their faces.'

It didn't take long for rumours to surface about what really happened the night Susan lost. Once backstage, there was what seemed like the beginning of a breakdown. Susan was said to have shouted, 'I hate this show. I hate it,' before allegedly running down the corridor in her bra and throwing a cup of water over a floor manager. Clearly no one had a clue what to do.

Susan's brother Gerry said, 'They just left her on her own. She has got a short fuse and she just blew. Who wouldn't under that pressure? She's told me, "I feel tired and stressed," and that's understandable.'

The production company played the whole thing down, merely admitting that Susan had had a few 'wobbles'. In certain quarters there was bemusement. After all, though it was disappointing that she hadn't won, she still had a career ahead of her, so why all the fuss? But that was to totally misunderstand the problems facing Susan. She had been part of a massive project, and now it had all come tumbling down and she found there were very few people to support her. There was talk of meeting with Simon Cowell the following week to discuss an album, but what Susan really needed was human comfort, and plenty of it.

Everyone knew that Susan had been deprived of oxygen at birth, but what they seemed reluctant to accept was that this behaviour was a direct result of that. As her neighbours in Blackburn had testified, she occasionally had fits of anger, even in a quiet Scottish village, far away from the stresses and strains of the showbusiness world, where Susan now found herself. She needed calm and compassion, strength and understanding, but instead she found herself surrounded by people who didn't know how to handle or comfort her.

What they did know, though, was that she needed professional help, and so Susan was taken to a doctor, who told her she needed complete rest. This was played down by those around her, with her spokesperson merely commenting, 'She has been seen by her private GP, who supports her decision to take a few days out for rest and recovery.' She was going to need a lot more than that, though.

At least Diversity were doing the decent thing and wishing her well. 'Susan was very gracious,' said the leader of the troupe, Ashley Banjo. 'She was really cool and so nice about it. She told us we were something special. Susan gave us big hugs and had a bit of a dance with us. There was a bit of poppin' and lockin'. She's a cool bird. Susan has become a superstar across the world, and to beat her is still a massive shock. We thought she was amazing on Saturday night, as always. She's going to have a great career.' It was hard to escape the conclusion that even they had mixed feelings about their win.

Matters escalated. No one would admit exactly what was going on behind the scenes, but it was known that Susan had been taken to The Priory clinic after fainting in front of production staff, and she was being treated there for exhaustion. Concern about what was happening to her had by now reached such a peak that there were suggestions that the makers of the show should face an inquiry. *Britain's Got Talent* and Syco, Cowell's entertainment company, were paying for her treatment, but continued to play the situation down: 'We provided Susan with a counsellor in the last week, when it became evident to us in the run-up to the final that she needed support.' That was putting it mildly.

Even Gordon Brown, the prime minister and a fellow Scot, found the need to comment on GMTV, 'I hope Susan Boyle is OK, because she is a really, really nice person.'

This did, at least, allow the more negative element of the public to see that those public spats were not Susan behaving like a diva, but a cry for help. Intensive debate raged about the morality of taking a fragile woman out of a close-knit community and exposing her to the glare of the worldwide media.

The question about the *Britain's Got Talent* tour had still not been resolved, and so Simon Cowell stepped in, saying, 'She won't be doing anything until she feels better.' He must have been worried, too, in case the situation rebounded badly on him.

Irene Carter, the mother of one of the members of the dance troupe Sugar Free, had seen what was happening close up.

'Susan was acting very strange all week,'

she told the *Daily Express.* 'One time, staff working on the show backstage asked if she was OK and she said she was talking to her friend. She then introduced everyone in the room to this "friend", who wasn't actually there. Another time she came up to my daughter Emma in the hotel and asked to borrow her mobile phone. She left this really bizarre message, which went on for several minutes. When she got off the phone she said she had been talking to her cat back at home.'

This was the last thing the programme makers needed: Susan's problems were beginning to look much worse than anyone had realized. The breast-beating in the press about whether she had been used as a pawn in a high-stakes commercial game continued, with fingers pointing at the amount of money various people stood to make out of this vulnerable woman.

Matters reached such a pitch that Talkback Thames, the company behind the programme, was forced to comment. 'It is a talent show at the end of the day, and people are auditioning on their talent merits,' said a spokeswoman. 'There is no formal psychological testing at the beginning of the show. Compared with something like *Big Brother,* where you are looking at people going into a house for three months, the people on *Britain's Got Talent* have three or four performances maximum and spend only seven to ten days in a hotel for the semi-finals and final. It is a very different scenario. But because of the level of media attention and the speed with which this has become a global phenomenon, we will be reviewing all of our policies in relation to psychological assessment.'

At least Susan was receiving proper treatment now. There had been reports that she had been sectioned, but that was not the case. She attended The Priory voluntarily by ambulance with, at her doctor's request, a police escort. And she was beginning to calm down. Her brother Gerry spoke to her. 'She's at The Priory, talking to people there about how she feels and where she goes from here,' he told the *Guardian*. 'She sounded a bit happier, she sounded a bit more like herself, but certainly a bit more rested. She's been on a tremendous roller-coaster. There's been an enormous amount of media speculation and intense activity. She's not used to that. She's coming to terms with that, now that she's no longer an anonymous face. I think what led up to it was the build-up to the show, and just psyching herself up for that, and then wondering after the show, "Where do I go now?" '

It was a question that still loomed large as matters remained in limbo. Susan recovered quite quickly, and with hindsight it's apparent that it wasn't a particularly serious episode. But at the time, no one knew how long she would be ill and what she would be able to manage in the immediate future. There was also the matter of the much-discussed album. Far from rushing something out in the immediate wake of the show, that would have to be more carefully paced.

The judges were trying to make the best of it. Both Piers and Amanda went on the record as saying that it was probably for the best that Susan didn't win, because the pressure on her would have been so great that her health might have suffered. In fact, if she had won, it would have provided her with the validation she craved, but there was no use brooding about that now.

Another element that had been played down by all concerned for fairly obvious reasons is that on the night of the final, Susan had to put up with something else she hadn't experienced before: booing. Piers apologized to her about it afterwards, and it was only a very small element of a large crowd, but to someone like Susan it must have been devastating.

To have had victory snatched away, then to hear the public, who had seemed to adore her, turning against her, must have totally undermined Susan's confidence. She had been treated cruelly, if not by the show itself, then by some members of the audience. Susan had had to put up with cruelty all her life, but this time it must have been particularly hard to bear.

After a day or so, matters took a turn for the better. It seemed that what Susan had suffered was an anxiety attack — extremely unpleasant and worrying at the time, but not, ultimately, serious. In addition, Susan's public was not deserting her. The president of the United States, Barack Obama, was said to want her to sing at celebrations for American Independence Day, and Susan was starting to fight back. 'I'm tired and I'm a wee bit homesick,' she was reported to have told her family. 'But I really hope I can still live the dream.'

Susan's brother Gerry, who was keeping a very close eye on events, told the *Daily Record* that Susan was fundamentally just homesick and missing Pebbles. And that the anxiety attack she'd experienced was just the fear that coming second would destroy her nascent career.

'She was sort of, "Where's it all going and what happens now?" Great things are made of the Royal Variety and plans for her career are still to be confirmed, but I asked her, "Seven weeks ago, if someone had told you that almost everyone in the world would know who you are, and you had a budding record contract and would never want for anything again, how would you have felt?" I told her, "This is not the end of your career — it's the start." This show has just been a launch pad. The world is waiting for Susan to release a record. I wonder how many established acts would love to have the opportunities she will have.' Gerry was spot on, and that was exactly what his sister needed to hear.

Any latent hostility to Susan that had built up in the week before the final had all but disappeared by now, and it was accepted that the reason she didn't respond normally to events, including the extraordinary circumstances she found herself in, was because she *couldn't.* Set against that was the fact that she'd been given the chance of a lifetime. Although her family was concerned about her, they were delighted that their sibling was going to have a chance to shine, indeed, although this was not to be the last nervous episode Susan experienced, she was making progress fast.

The *Britain's Got Talent* tour was about to kick off less than two weeks after the final, and was getting closer every day. Already, it was almost entirely sold out; indeed a further seven dates had been added due to popular demand. There was no doubt about why: the public wanted to see Susan. Whether she'd won or not, she was still the biggest draw. But no one had any idea whether or not she'd be strong enough to take part in the tour.

The whole thing was turning into a nightmare for the tour organizers, although everyone was adamant that Susan's health was paramount. Gerry pointed out that the best cure for Susan was for her to see that she was in as much demand as ever. It was, after all, fear that her career would be taken away from her before it had even begun that had put her in this state.

Amanda was keen to point out that Susan was in The Priory because she was 'knackered' rather than suffering from any underlying health issues, and that she would soon be fit again. As for Susan, well, she wasn't saying anything publicly. She just wanted to get well again.

Although Susan was temporarily off the scene, the circus surrounding her showed no sign of slowing down, and more and more opportunities for her to perform kept arising. Susan's brother John revealed that Sir Andrew Lloyd Webber, no less, had been in touch, although his sister's health meant that nothing more could be done about it yet.

Another offer of support came from an unexpected quarter — Elaine Paige. Elaine was the woman Susan had said she wanted to emulate, and she too had become famous almost overnight, after she starred in *Evita*. She quite clearly felt genuine concern for Susan.

'I really want to meet her as soon as I can,' she told the *Daily Express*. 'I hope I might be able to visit Susan when she is feeling up to it as I have so much advice I want to give her. I want to tell her to stay away from everything for a while and everyone connected with that show. She really needs to go home, get her head down and keep quiet. That is the only way she is going to get herself sorted out. I feel I have some very useful things to say to her. I have plenty of advice that I could give her based on my own experience. It was difficult enough for me when I starred in *Evita* in 1978, but this lady is from West Lothian and the media hype these days is much worse than it was back then. These days people who become famous face a total onslaught and she has had a hundred times more of it than I did because of YouTube and globalization. It would be difficult for anyone to deal with.'

But the fact remained Susan didn't want to have nothing to do with anyone on the show. *Britain's Got Talent* had given her the opportunity of a lifetime, and what she wanted more than anything was to get back out there. The offers were coming in thick and fast, and she wanted to be able to accept at least some of them and get back out on the road. After all, Barack Obama and Sir Andrew Lloyd Webber were not names to be sniffed at.

In the end, Susan's stay in The Priory lasted only a few days. There was yet more frenzied speculation about how she was being treated — one minute it was reported that her cat Pebbles would be brought in to surprise her, the next it was said that The Priory wouldn't allow Pebbles to visit because it was against the rules. Whatever the rumours, Susan left looking and feeling considerably better. This would not be the end of her troubles, but this particular episode was over with.

After she left the Priory, Susan did the best possible thing: she flew back to Scotland, where she was reunited with Pebbles, her family and friends. It had been a tumultuous time, and Susan had paid a heavy price for establishing herself. She might have been having problems, but she was turning into a star, and that was what she really wanted.

Given Susan's background and personal issues, it seems remarkable that matters didn't turn out considerably worse. But Susan was far more resilient than she was being given credit for, and whatever issues she might have had, she knew an opportunity when she saw one. Her life had changed beyond all recognition, and while there might have been a downside, there was a seriously big upside to the life that lay ahead. Susan Boyle had been tried and tested, and now she was on her way.

Susan's beloved mother, Bridget, posing with Mary Boyle (*left*) and Bridie Boyle (*right*).

Susan's father, Patrick Boyle, during his service in the Royal Engineers during the Second World War.

Susan and her family. Back row left to right: Gerard, James, John, Kathleen, Joe, Bridie, Mary. Front row left to right: Susan, Patrick (father) and Bridget (mother).

Susan's home
in Blackburn,
near Broxburn,
West Lothian.

Fred O'Neil, who
gave Susan singing
lessons for several
years and nurtured
her incredible talent.

Singing has
always been
Susan's passion!

Shots of Susan at home taken during the *Britain's Got Talent* series.

The formidable *Britain's Got Talent* judges. Left to right: Piers Morgan, Amanda Holden and Simon Cowell.

A woman viewing the incredible YouTube video clip of Susan's first performance of 'I Dreamed a Dream' on *Britain's Got Talent*.

In the run-up to the final, bookmakers were in a flurry of activity as the public placed bets on the final few contestants. Susan was the firm favourite at Ladbroke's bookmakers in her home town.

As the series reached its finale, it was clear that the most serious threat to Susan's victory was the brilliantly gymnastic dance troupe, Diversity.

However, if Ant and Dec, the show's jovial hosts, had the inside scoop on which way the audience was going to vote in the final, they certainly weren't letting on.

The support Susan received from the public was incredible.

Supporters wearing Susan masks gather in her hometown to watch the final of *Britain's Got Talent*.

Susan greets young fans at the door of her house.

Susan poses with two fans, Mathew Balderston and Kevin Hepworth, who drove for three hours from Alloa in order to meet their hero.

Susan wows fans during the opening show of the *Britain's Got Talent* live tour at the National Indoor Arena in Birmingham, in front of a packed audience of 5,000.

Susan smiles for the cameras with her doctor, Sarah Latzof, after her brief stay at The Priory.

Susan getting ready to board a plane from Heathrow Airport . . .

. . . and arriving at Los Angeles International Airport on her first trip to America.

Susan's beloved cat, Pebbles, became a celebrity in her own right – here, she's shielded from the snapping lights of photographers!

Susan performing as a guest on *America's Got Talent*. In her US TV singing debut, she covered the Rolling Stones track 'Wild Horses', as well as singing 'I Dreamed a Dream', the song that originally catapulted her to fame in the UK.

As part of its *People of the Year* show, NBC took a look at the most fascinating, inspirational and heroic figures of 2009. Susan was invited to appear as a guest and was interviewed by Matt Lauer.

Susan is greeted by throngs of fans when she arrives at JFK Airport, New York.

More fans gather to watch Susan perform at *The Today Show* in New York.

Susan takes to the stage at *The Today Show*, revels in the limelight and delights the audience.

Back home in Blackburn after her incredible US trip, Susan poses in her dressing gown for the photographers gathered outside her house, hoping to catch a glimpse of her new, post-makeover look.

Susan was to capture the hearts of not just Britain and America, but the whole world. She has appeared on major chat shows throughout Europe. Here she poses with French television presenter Michel Drucker.

As part of her trip to Europe, Susan performs on German television show *Menschen 2009*.

German television presenter Thomas Gottschalk presents a bouquet of flowers to Susan after her performance on the show.

Susan returns to her home in Blackburn. She may have triumphantly conquered the world, but home is still very much where her heart is.

THE SPECIAL CHILD

Britain, 1961. The decade that was to change the world was getting underway, and as the 1960s progressed, all the old certainties were torn down, rocking the establishment and ripping apart and rebuilding the foundations of society. It was the decade that would usher in Swinging London, riots in Paris, flower power and the summer of love; and it would produce revolutionary new musical talents, such as The Beatles, the Rolling Stones, Cream, the Velvet Underground, the New Faces and many more.

Above all, though, it offered opportunity. Britain's rigid class system came tumbling down, and for the first time ever it became fashionable to be working class. Luminaries of the era included working-class Londoners Michael Caine, Roger Moore, Terence Stamp, Twiggy and David Bailey. All of them came from humble backgrounds, and all of them became globally famous icons of the decade they came to represent.

Far away from London, in the small Scottish mining village of Blackburn, this revolution was passing by almost unnoticed. There, life went on much as it had done for decades, with hard work and bringing up your family as priorities. Blackburn was a small, traditional community, a world away from the bright lights and big city that its most famous daughter was one day going to experience: life could be hard, but you didn't complain, you got on with it.

That, then, was the background against which Susan was brought up. It was to be many years before she, too, would prosper in the new modern Britain, and by the time she did so, Britain would have gone through yet another revolution, the digital revolution. It was this digital revolution — and the birth of the internet and websites such as YouTube — that were to play a huge and pivotal role in her success. To Susan, who at the time she was discovered did not own a computer, this whole phenomenon was new. It wouldn't be long before she adapted, though.

Back in 1961, the Boyles were already a large family when it was announced that another surprise addition was on the way.

Indeed, the Boyle family, first generation immigrants from County Donegal in Ireland, was almost complete. Patrick, a miner who went on to become a store man at the British Leyland factory in Bathgate, and who was also a World War II veteran, to say nothing of being an amateur singer in his spare time, and his wife Bridget, a shorthand typist, were getting ready for the birth of their tenth child.

On 1 April 1961, Susan Magdalane Boyle arrived, the youngest of four brothers and six sisters. A surprise child, she was the youngest by six years. Bridget was forty-seven by now, and unfortunately there were problems during the birth. The baby was briefly deprived of oxygen during labour, and this led to problems that would affect the child — Susan — throughout her life.

Susan knew from the word go what had happened to her, and she was also aware, at the beginning at least, that not a great deal was expected of her.

'When I was a baby they didn't really give me much scope because they told my parents not to expect too much of me and just play things by ear because I had a slight disability,' she told the *Sunday Express*. Despite this, though, Susan was a much-loved child and grew up the apple of her parents', and particularly her mother's, eye.

At home, life was happy. The family was packed into the house where Susan lives to this day, which became a place full of children shrieking and hollering, rough and tumbling. At home, Susan wasn't treated any differently from anyone else, and the shyness that crippled her out of doors was nowhere to be seen.

'I was a cheeky little girl at home,' Susan told the *Sunday Times.* 'You had to fight your corner in a family the size of ours.' But outside it was a different matter. Susan's learning difficulties set her apart from the other children, and, as so often happens in cases like this, she was bullied. It did not make for an easy life.

'I was born with a disability and that made me a target for bullies,' she told the *Sunday Mirror.* 'I was called names because of my fuzzy hair and because I struggled in class.

'I told the teachers but, because it was more verbal than physical, I could never prove anything. But words often hurt more than cuts and bruises and the scars are still there. I still see the kids I went to school with, because we all live in the same area. They're all grown up with children of their own. But look at me now — I've got the

154

last laugh.'

She had indeed, but that didn't make it any easier to deal with at the time. If anything, it made Susan's problems worse, because, as she later related as an adult, it caused anger to build up inside her, an anger that had nowhere to go. Those occasions when she lashed out in public as an adult can be directly attributed to the problems she endured as a child, when there was no one to help or defend her. Once away from her family, who were extremely protective, Susan was forced to fend for herself. No one in authority helped her, if indeed they even realized what was going on. And so the anger kept growing, becoming increasingly internalized. No wonder it burst out in the end.

Susan's talent for singing emerged early on. Her father, Patrick, had sung on wartime radio, so there was clearly an aptitude for singing in the family.

'We're all singers in our family, but I think we get our voices from him,' Susan said. 'I joke that my mum knew I had a good pair of lungs when I used to bawl as a baby. But it was really when I was about twelve and I started singing in school productions and in the choir. The teachers said I had a talent, but I was too young to know.'

Singing also started to provide a refuge from other elements of life, and it played an increasingly big role in her life when she moved into her teens.

Susan's singing had begun several years earlier, before she started to take part in school productions, but although she was a member of some choirs, Susan tended to fade into the background when she sang with them. A child as shy as Susan was always going to find it difficult to step into the limelight, and so it proved to be.

'I've sung since I was about nine,' she told the American magazine *TV Guide*. 'I'd do theatrical stuff and join choirs. I was picked for a solo once, but choirs for me were about hiding behind other people. They were about taking comfort in letting other people take the lead. I was quite shy back then. Hard to believe after everything that's happened this year, I know! But I was. By the time you get to my age, you lose that shyness.'

Susan's brother Gerard, who was six years her senior and the closest to her in age, said much the same. 'My father sang in working men's clubs and so did I,' he told the *Sunday Mirror*. 'We're a very musical family and would all have a sing-song at weddings and family occasions. But Susan was so shy she'd take a back seat. It was only when she was about ten she sang at a family wedding and we realized she had a real talent. After that we couldn't stop her.' In private, that is. To the outside world Susan remained very much the bashful little girl.

It wasn't just Susan who was singing, though; the whole family was at it. As Susan recalled to *TV Guide,* 'Oh, we were quite a squad, all with different abilities, but all very musical,' she said. 'My brother Joe was a songwriter, too. My dad used to sing. My mother sung and played piano. I have two sisters that are very good singers. We were a wee bit like the Von Trapps! There were guitars sitting about the house, and a piano, and we'd all experiment with them. We loved the Beatles in the Sixties. I was just a wee lassie and we'd sit and watch *Top of the Pops* and wait for them and the Rolling Stones to come on. My dad hated that programme, so he used to turn it down. I used to turn it up just for devilment.'

Ironically, Susan has gone on to sing a Rolling Stones number on her album, eliciting praise from Mick Jagger himself. Such an outcome would have seemed unimaginable to the little girl.

Were Susan to have been born today, it is

possible that someone would have realized that her musical ability was a way of compensating for the problems she had experienced, using it as a way of communicating with the world. But this was a small village in Scotland in the 1960s, and it didn't occur to anyone that this might be Susan's way of making her mark on the world. Instead, she was simply acknowledged as an odd little thing, who didn't really fit in with anyone else, and who was destined for an existence on the sidelines of life. The thought of a singing career as such would have been inconceivable, and it was this attitude that prevailed well into Susan's adulthood, and against which she had to fight in order to achieve success.

As Susan grew up, the fact that she was a little different from the other children in the village isolated her even more. Although as an adult there were many people in the village who would befriend her and watch out for her, as a child that wasn't the case. Instead, she lived an increasingly isolated life, as her concerned parents observed her inability to form close bonds with other children and to indulge in the only uncomplicated pleasure she had: music. It would seem that because she couldn't make friends easily, music assumed an ever more important role in her life.

'Susan was what you would call a loner,' said Gerard. 'She was happiest on her own, playing her records and losing herself in music. She didn't really interact with other children. She was seen as different because she didn't have the same interests as kids her age. As a teenager she was never into make-up or boys. She was easily upset. She'd take nasty comments literally, so found it hard to make friends or develop relationships outside the family. Eventually she retreated into her own world. Music became her thing.'

All this puts her outbursts as an adult into context: Susan had simply never learned to cope with the more brutal aspects of the outside world. A sensitive child, she grew into a sensitive woman, who never acquired the outer carapace that most people develop to help them deal with the world. And there was also her crippling shyness to cope with. Susan was aware that she was different from most people, but she didn't know how to deal with that fact. In addition, she didn't possess the social know-how necessary when it comes to interacting with others, and so her isolation continued as she moved into her teens.

Like a lot of girls at the time, the teenage

Susan fell for the charms of toothsome Donny Osmond (who she would later meet), who was beyond doubt the biggest male heartthrob in Britain in the early Seventies. And so, for the first time, Susan began to associate love with music, and as a result her passion for singing grew greater still.

'When she was a girl, she was obsessed with Donny Osmond,' Gerard recalled. 'His posters were all over her walls. She would lock herself in her room and play the records over and over again, singing along as loud as possible. It used to drive me mad when I would hear it start up the hundredth time. But our mum would say, "Leave her alone, it's all she's got." Looking back now, I realize that was how she honed her skills, as she'd stand in front of the mirror in her bedroom for hours singing the songs until she'd achieved perfection.'

Another of Susan's favourites was one of the smash hits of the era, *Grease,* and she would sing those songs, too. As an adult, Susan knew that her teenage infatuation with Donny, and her obsession with his music, provided her with something the rest of life could not.

'It was a complete emotional release,' she said. 'I had a slight disability . . . and I had to find my abilities and concentrate on that instead. Singing was the one thing that I was good at. Music was my escape, and my brother bought me lots of LPs. I was daft about the Osmonds at the time. I used to go up to my bedroom and play records. I could be who I wanted to be. I used to imagine myself singing to an audience. It was my safe haven. Even at thirteen, I would see people singing on the TV and wanted to be in that position and entertain people.'

But as Susan was beginning to harbour the dream she would only realize in later life, school was not providing a great deal of help. Some of the teachers were sympathetic, encouraging her to get involved in the school's dramatic productions, but many were not. One of the worst and least talked about aspects of child bullying is that it isn't uncommon for a teacher to join in. Once a pack of animals — for that is what bullies are — senses weakness, the herd mentality kicks in, so instead of being encouraged to pursue the obvious talent she possessed, Susan found herself on the receiving end of brutality instead.

'I was often left behind at school because of one thing or another,' Susan explained as an adult, sounding remarkably equable about the treatment she'd received. 'I'm just a wee bit slower at picking things up than other people, so you get left behind in a system that just wants to rush on. That was what I felt was happening to me. And this feels like a good way of making up for that. I don't think the resources were there for me back then at school. Teachers have more specialized training now. There was discipline for the sake of discipline back then, and you are looking at someone who would get the belt every day. "Will you shut up, Susan!" Whack! But the majority of my childhood was quite happy, until I started getting bullied. There's nothing worse than another person having power over you by bullying you and you not knowing how to get rid of that thing.'

She was right: these days she'd have been sent to a special needs school, where she'd be taught by teachers who'd been properly trained to look after someone with her problems. As it was, a combination of beating and bullying was no way to bring out the artiste in anyone. In fact it had quite the opposite effect, causing Susan to retreat even deeper into her shell. The wonder is that she ever managed to get out of it, for when Susan finally set out to achieve her destiny, she showed a determination and energy she wouldn't have been credited with in those early days. All that, though, was still some way off.

As Susan grew up, despite her crush on Donny, no real-life boyfriend emerged, although she was to have a very brief romance later, of which more anon. Her parents were concerned that someone might take advantage of their child, and so potential suitors were held at bay.

'My parents didn't want me to have boyfriends so I've never been on a date,' Susan said more recently. 'I suppose I've accepted it's never going to happen. The only thing I really do regret is not having children. I love kids and would like to have been a mum.'

Looking at pictures of the young Susan, it's entirely possible it might have happened had she met the right man. Susan may have had wild, frizzy hair, but when she combed it she was a very pretty girl. It was her stultifying shyness that really put paid to any chance of romance, that and the fact that she would never have defied her parents.

And so Susan moved towards young womanhood with no romance on the cards, and not a great deal else either.

■ ■ ■ ■

Susan's brothers and sisters were all much older than her, and so they began to move away from the little house in Blackburn, in one case emigrating to Australia, while Susan stayed on with her parents. She left school aged seventeen with few qualifications, and went on to take her one and only job, as a trainee chef in the kitchen of a West Lothian college. It didn't last long. 'It was a six-month contract and then it stopped,' she said. She also enrolled in various government training schemes, but none of them came to anything. In all honesty, no one expected Susan to have a career: as the unmarried daughter, she was expected to stay at home and look after her parents. Nor did Susan question this. To this day she classifies herself as the 'wee wifey with a mop'.

But although Susan went unnoticed, her voice did not. Part of the powerful appeal of her story is that, in middle age, she appeared to spring out of nowhere with an astonishing gift, but in actual fact there was more to it than that. Susan had begun going to musicals in Edinburgh, which is where she first saw *Les Miserables* at the Playhouse. It was a show she fell in love with straight away — 'It took my breath away,' she said — and would go on to provide her with a massive opportunity in the form of her audition song 'I Dreamed A Dream' in the years to come.

Aware of Susan's formidable gifts, her mother Bridget encouraged her to participate in local talent shows, and Susan attended Edinburgh Acting School, although at this point a career on the stage would have seemed too far-fetched even to contemplate. She was also still needed at home, though, and Susan eventually gave up and returned to Blackburn to care for her parents.

At least she had made an appearance on the Edinburgh Fringe, and in addition a seed had been planted in her mind. Susan began to perform at local venues and on family occasions, so much so that by the time she made it on to *Britain's Got Talent,* she was quite well known locally for the beauty of her voice. The nation may have been staggered by what it heard on *BGT,* but West Lothian wasn't.

Susan was also taking lessons with a voice coach, Fred O'Neil, a relationship that continues to this day, although there was a gap of several years when Susan stopped singing after her mother died.

■ ■ ■ ■

Most of the travelling that Susan did before she became famous entailed trips to France and Ireland, and singing was a part of those trips, too. Susan and her family often went to Mayo's Knock Shrine in Ireland, where she sang at the basilica in the Marian Shrine, as a member of the annual Legion of Mary pilgrimage from Our Lady of Lourdes, Susan's local church in Blackburn.

Everyone in Mayo was as astounded by her voice as her friends back home, and they were just as thrilled by her later success. They knew from first hand how the judges felt when they first heard her sing.

'When I watched the judges' faces, it reminded me of what I was like when I first saw Susan singing,' said her parish priest Father Basil Clark. 'I was absolutely blown away by the quality of the singing and by that fantastic voice. Anyone who sees her for the first time behaves the same way. I have never heard her sing badly, though she might lose the words if the stress gets too much. When she gets up to sing it can either be wonderful or you can get the unpredictable eccentric behaviour, but it is to do with the fact that she has learning difficulties. In a sense, there is a beautiful voice trapped in this damaged body. It is an absolute contrast. There she was on television, acting very peculiarly, and the audience was expecting peculiar things to happen and then the voice of an angel comes out — and that's Susan.'

At some stage in all this — Susan didn't specify dates — Susan had her one and only relationship to date. It didn't go very far physically, but for a brief while it seemed that it might turn serious as an engagement was discussed. In the wake of her audition for *Britain's Got Talent,* Susan had seemed a little embarrassed about her throwaway line about never having been kissed, saying that she had only been joking, and it is true that she had had a very gentle introduction into the world of romance. It wasn't to last, though.

'I had a boyfriend, John,' she told the *Daily Mirror.* 'He asked me to marry him after seven weeks. We went to visit his mum and she started telling me what our kitchen was going to be like when we got married! Even what fridge we could have, although we'd only ever had a peck on the cheek! He got cold feet. It made me sad, in a way. It makes you feel unattractive. You feel that life is passing you by. But I thought, Maybe

167

there's something for me later. I was always optimistic.'

Poor Susan. In truth, little was running smoothly for her back then. But by this time the exceptional quality of her voice meant that she was beginning to consider a career as a professional singer, despite all the setbacks she'd encountered in her life to date. The question was, how would she achieve this?

From a background like Susan's, there are few obvious routes into the world of show-business, especially when you don't conform to the norm of what a person should look like. As Susan got older, she was starting to neglect her appearance, for the simple reason that she didn't care about it and couldn't see why anyone else should. Even her family affectionately called her Worzel Gummidge, and while this might not have mattered when she was young and pretty, as Susan got older it began to take its toll.

'She has never been bothered about her appearance,' said Gerard. 'She doesn't wear make-up or fancy clothes. It's not that she doesn't care, she just doesn't see why other people should care how she looks. When me or my sisters see her we always say, "Och Susan, you could have put a comb through your hair." But she can't see what the problem is.'

It was a laudable attitude, but one that was to hold her back, because in this shallow, superficial world of ours, people judge you on what they see, and nowhere more so than in showbusiness. Susan was at least a little aware of that, because in 1995, at the age of thirty-three, she made her first real attempt at a breakthrough when she auditioned for Michael Barrymore's show *My Kind of People.* She looked considerably smarter than she did in her audition for *Britain's Got Talent,* wearing a bright pink cardigan and with her hair tightly pulled back.

Difficult as it is to remember now, in 1995, Michael Barrymore was one of the most popular entertainers in the country. That was actually the year he came out and split from his wife Cheryl, an event that precipitated the subsequent decline of his career. At the time, however, one of the hallmarks of his show was the rapport he had with his audience and the people who appeared on the show. He would clown around and tease them, which is the only explanation for the way he behaved towards Susan Boyle.

As mentioned earlier in the book, a video exists of this encounter, which took place at the Olympia Shopping Centre in East Kilbride. The short clip — only a minute and a half long — has been posted online, and the camera is mainly directed towards Barrymore, who is clowning around in the background, rather than on Susan herself. She is singing 'I Don't Know How To Love Him' from *Jesus Christ Superstar,* and the clarity and purity of her voice comes across well, though Barrymore doesn't appear to notice.

He is seen talking and gesticulating in the background, before lying down on the ground and pushing himself towards Susan in an attempt to look up her skirt. Seemingly unruffled, Susan attempts to kick him away before bending down to sing to him. Barrymore doesn't initially engage, but as they both stand up, he leans into the microphone to sing the last few words with her, before grabbing the startled woman and embracing her. It's a clip that, if nothing else, proves that Susan had, in fact, been kissed.

At the time, that was the end of that. Susan didn't make it on to the show, and the incident would have been totally forgotten about had she not gone on to achieve global fame fourteen years later. The moment she became a sensation, however, the clip was posted on YouTube and Barrymore got the belated rubbishing he deserved.

'Typical Barrymore,' read one typical post. 'I remember this show and I remember if anyone had any talent at all he started to mess. He hated to be upstaged and to be shown as the talentless hack he truly is. Well look who's laughing now.'

'What an arse!' said another. 'Trying to steal the show away from the real talent of Susan in such a vulgar way.'

One correspondent pointed out that after an experience like that, Susan was doubly brave to risk humiliation again: 'How much courage did it take for her to appear on *Britain's Got Talent*?' read the post. 'When you consider this experience, I think a great deal of courage, indeed.'

Susan herself was dismissive of the episode in the wake of her appearance on *Britain's Got Talent*. 'I did *My Kind of People* for fun,' she said. 'I also sang locally, but things had quietened down.'

The producers of *My Kind of People* certainly missed a trick, for in hindsight, one of the great mysteries about Susan was that it took so long for anyone to discover her. She was becoming increasingly well known in her immediate neighbourhood, and everyone who saw her sing was awestruck. In addition to singing in karaoke competitions in the pub, she sang in church, at family occasions and when any other opportunity arose. It would seem the only reason her talent remained hidden was that Susan didn't fit the conventional view of what and who a singer should be.

A few years later, there was another chance for her to be discovered when a charity record on which she sang was made. Susan's life at this stage seems to be a never-ending stream of people missing what was right under their nose, namely Susan's amazing voice, for even when they did hear it, they didn't realize its commercial appeal, although admittedly in this case at least someone tried to market her formidable talent. Sadly, though, it didn't go any further at this point.

The Millennium Celebration disc was a compilation CD for charity, recorded in 1999 at Whitburn Academy where, coincidentally, *X Factor* winner Leon Jackson had been a pupil. The idea had come from Eddie Anderson, a local newspaper editor, and funds had been forthcoming from Whitburn Community Council. They then held auditions, as Eddie was looking for previously undiscovered artists to take part.

Susan duly auditioned and knocked everyone out. 'I was amazed when she sang,' said Eddie in the wake of her triumph on *Britain's Got Talent.* 'It was probably the same reaction as everyone had last Saturday. Susan was exactly the same then as she is now. She has a fabulous and unique talent.'

Susan recorded 'Cry Me A River' for the CD, of which only 1,000 copies were made, making it something of a collector's item today. Amazingly, despite the number of people who now knew what an extraordinary voice she had, it was to be a full decade before she finally got her big break. There was a lot of dark muttering to the effect that the makers of *Britain's Got Talent* knew exactly what they were doing when they put Susan on the stage, but the fact is that, with almost no encouragement, Susan had put herself forward for years before anyone paid any attention to what she could do. One endeavour after another came to nothing, with no one taking her seriously, and to make matters worse, Susan had to put up with the loutish antics of people like Michael Barrymore.

What is really unbelievable is that with so little encouragement, other than from her mother, Susan had the drive and ambition to battle on. Much has been made of her learning difficulties, but what really stands out is her determination and self-belief. Simon Cowell might have been the man to finally put her on the global map, but it was Susan herself who embarked on the journey.

But before she got there, there was to be even more pain and heartbreak.

TRAGEDY
AND TRIUMPH

By her late thirties, it was beginning to seem as if Susan's big break would never happen. She appeared to have tried all the avenues of opportunity open to her, and had got nowhere. In the late 1990s, she made what must have seemed like her last big effort, using all her savings to record a demo tape, on which she sang 'Cry Me A River' and Roberta Flack's hit 'Killing Me Softly'. She distributed this CD to a handful of friends, but if it was meant to break down barriers, it didn't do the trick. Like the Millennium Celebration CD, it is now, of course, a collector's item, but at the time it didn't help her make inroads into the record business.

And so began a very difficult time for Susan. In 1999 she lost her father, and 18 months later her sister Kathleen, to whom Susan had been very close, also passed away. It shook Susan badly. 'Kathleen's death hit Susan very hard,' her brother

Gerard told the *Sunday Mirror*. 'Susan was very close to her and Kathleen doted on Susan. Kathleen suffered an asthma attack at home in 2000. Obviously losing Dad was hard, but at least he was older and he'd lived his life.'

It must have felt like the end of an era as Susan's world contracted around her rather than expanded. To lose two people who had been so close to her in such a short period of time was devastating, not least because they were both her protectors. In her early years, Susan might have had her problems, but at least she had a family who protected her; now that was less and less the case. While Susan's other siblings loved and cared about their sister, they were getting married and having families of their own — they had other concerns at the centre of their lives.

Susan lived a quiet life, caring for her mother and working as a volunteer at Our Lady of Lourdes, where she would visit older members of the congregation several times a week. 'I wasn't working, so we scraped by on mum's pension and my benefits,' she told the *Daily Record*. 'It was a sad time, but I was happy at home. My parents always thought it was better I lived with them so they could keep me safe.

That's why I've never been on a date or met a man. My mum and dad didn't want me to have boyfriends because they were worried they would try and take advantage of me. Time went on and I just accepted it was never going to happen.'

It was a frugal existence, though. Susan and her mother had always been close, but now circumstances were such that the bond between them grew stronger still. With just the two of them living in what had once been home to a family of twelve, increasingly the two had only each other for emotional comfort. It must have been extremely worrying for Bridget, who knew that no one would be there to look after Susan once she had gone. Susan had never left home, never lived on her own and never, apart from a brief six months in her teens, had a job of any description. Her siblings were around to keep an eye out for her, of course, and the local church would always be there, but Bridget must have been concerned. Consequently, she did as much as she could during the last few years of her life to ensure her daughter would be materially comfortable. She did the house up as much as possible, knowing, perhaps, that Susan would have less interest in looking after her surroundings, and prepared for what was to come.

'Before she got very ill, she began putting money aside for me, and got nice carpets for the house and stuff like that,' Susan later recalled. 'I'd ask her what she was buying it for and she said, "Susan, I'm not going to be with you much longer. I'm getting old." I still couldn't follow her. It wasn't until she went that it sunk in.'

Bridget died in 2007, leading to the darkest time in Susan's life. She was forty-five and had formed an intensely strong bond with her mother, without having created a family of her own, like her siblings. After all those decades of struggling to get noticed, Susan found herself totally alone, with no husband, no career, and seemingly nothing to look forward to. The future must have looked bleak indeed.

It took Susan a while for the full implications of what had happened to sink in, and she recalled how it was at the very end: 'In February 2007, [Mum] was taken into hospital suffering from dehydration,' Susan told the *Daily Mail.* 'Obviously she was dying. She wasn't aware of her surroundings. She looked completely different. I couldn't imagine that shell of a woman was my mother. She was a beautiful person, very warm and kind and very articulate.

'It's a very unusual experience, watching someone you love go. When people die, they just go to sleep. I held her hand and, a few minutes before she went, I don't know what it was, but she smiled at something she saw. I don't know whether it was Our Lady or my dad, but whoever it was, it was as if she was saying, "It's all right." She was in bliss, in a kind of limbo, a wee world of her own. I can talk about it now, but I couldn't have done a year or so ago. I'd have been too emotional.'

It took Susan a long time to come to terms with the loss of her mother. The comfort of Bridget's final moments, in which she appeared to be in a state of bliss, did not last, for now Susan was well and truly alone. Her faith helped her to find what consolation she could, and she still had her cat Pebbles, but however much you love a pet, it cannot make up for the loss of a parent, particularly one with whom you share such a strong bond. Susan was devastated. Now there was no one to come home to and no one to ward off the more unpleasant elements of the village, who used to make life difficult for Susan.

Susan recalls a very black time: 'I was very lonely and very upset,' she remembered afterwards, explaining that it took quite a while before she felt strong enough even to talk about it. 'There was a kind of numbness to begin with, because you don't know what's happening, but then it hit me like a ton of bricks. My health went down. I had panic attacks and felt I couldn't cope. I didn't eat or sleep properly. I'd had everything done for me. But the rest of my family helped pull me through. I think I still struggle with my independence a bit, because I depended on my mother so much — although I have a lot more help nowadays.'

It was Susan's dependence on her mother that made the loss so hard to deal with. Essentially, in many ways, Susan had never been allowed to grow up. Because she'd never gone through the stage that most adults do of breaking away to find a life of their own, she had never established an identity as an independent grown-up, and now she was being called upon to do so for the first time in the most painful circumstances. Her Catholicism helped, but even so the loss was keenly felt.

'When I walk into the house now, I'm lonely,' she said in the aftermath of the audition. 'But this is where my faith comes in. Her physical presence is no longer here, but

180

her spirit is. She's still very much a part of me — she's in my heart. To hang on to her memory is good, in a way, but in another way it's not so good, because you don't get on with your own life, and my mother wouldn't have wanted that.'

In the immediate aftermath of Bridget's death, Susan went into a state of shock, and so it took some time for the loss to sink in. It is common in the immediate aftermath of a death for it to take some time before the reality of what has happened to set in, and so it was to prove with Susan. Initially, of course, there was the funeral to organize, arrangements to be made and the house to sort out: the sheer weight of duty and protocol that must be adhered to after someone has died. In the aftermath of her loss, Susan was left on her own to brood about what had happened and where her life was going. Real feelings of isolation set in.

'After mum died it didn't fully register until maybe six months after, when the loneliness set in and there was nobody except my cat,' she told the *Daily Record.* 'When you lose someone as powerful as your mum, you feel as if a part of you is taken away and it does things to your confidence. My confidence was pretty down at that time. I told myself that, though she's not here physically, mentally and spiritually she is. That's what keeps you going. I have my faith, which is the backbone of who I am.'

In the immediate aftermath of Bridget's death, on top of everything she'd had to deal with, something else catastrophic happened. For the first time in her life, Susan lost her voice. The combined results of shock and grief meant that Susan's best way of communicating with the outside world was closed to her. Just as her neighbours would later testify that they saw very little of Susan during this dark time, because she couldn't bear to see people, so it seems she could no longer bear to use the great gift that would one day bring her so much. Bridget had always encouraged Susan to sing, all the way back to when she was a little girl, and to engage in an activity so closely associated with her mother now that she had passed away made it even more painful. 'For a while after my mother's death I wasn't able to sing,' said Susan. 'I was too upset. I stayed at home, did the housework, day-to-day tasks.'

Ultimately, though, Susan came to see the gift that she'd been given — her beautiful voice — as a way of reconnecting with her mother and, eventually, fulfilling the dreams her mother had had for her . . . but not yet. The rawness of the emotions she was feeling was too much to bear, silencing her temporarily. And it wasn't just grief she was feeling — although that was a huge part of it — it was isolation too. At the time, Susan must have felt as if she would never be free of the burden of unhappiness she was carrying, and as though she had reached the limit of what life had to offer her.

Her family was aware of what she was going through. 'It was easier for the rest of us because we had husbands, wives and partners, but Susan was on her own,' said Gerard. 'It was just her left in the family home, which had gone from a hive of activity over the years down to just her. But as time has gone on Susan has got stronger. She realizes Mum has gone now and has come to terms with it and taken strength from that.'

The despair Susan felt in the wake of her mother's death combined with the despair she felt about where her life was going. It was not just a case of not being able to sing: she didn't *want* to sing, either. All those dreams of being another Elaine Paige had come to nothing — Susan had done as much as she could, and she didn't have the energy to try anymore. There was a feeling that this was it: this was what her life had amounted to. All the promise of youth and her beautiful voice had come to nothing. There was nothing to hope for anymore.

This was confirmed by those who knew her. 'She always had a vision of herself as a singer, but last year she told me she wasn't going to sing any more,' her voice coach Fred O'Neil told the *Sunday Times* in the wake of Susan's triumph on *Britain's Got Talent*. 'I remember a phone call late last year when she said she was too old and that it was a young person's game.' But Fred had been training her for the longer term: 'When I first heard her sing, it was obvious she had a naturally good voice and our work was to make sure it lasted a lifetime and that it was extended to its full capacity,' he continued. 'That [the audition] was her just gearing up, she can sing better than that.'

She was in no state to do so back then, though; as far as Susan was concerned, it was all over. But into even the blackest grief and despair, some light eventually shines, and so it was with Susan. After a period of intense suffering, she began to look at life in a different way. The raw grief was mellowing into acceptance, and Susan was beginning to think about what her mother had really meant to her, and what Bridget had encouraged her to do. And what Bridget had wanted was for Susan to sing.

Not only that, she wanted Susan to get out there and show the world what she could do. Yes, Susan had made some earlier attempts to get noticed, but Bridget didn't want her to give up. She didn't think Susan was too old, and she believed she had a good chance of arousing people's interest. In addition, Bridget was a great fan of talent shows such as *The X Factor* — *Britain's Got Talent* aired for the first time shortly after her death — and she thought her daughter should give it a go.

'Mum loved the show and used to tell me I should put my name down and that I'd win it if I did,' Susan told the *Daily Mail*. 'But I never thought I was good enough. It was only after she died that I plucked up the courage to enter. It was a very dark time and I suffered depression and anxiety. But out of the darkness came light. I realized I wanted to make her proud of me, and the only way to do that was to take the risk and enter the show.'

By entering the show — although it would be *Britain's Got Talent,* rather than *The X Factor* — Susan would be re-establishing a relationship with her mother and fulfilling

185

Bridget's ambitions for her. And so from the depths of despair arose new drive and determination. If Bridget had thought she was good enough to be on the programme then, as an act of love for her mother, Susan would prove her right.

Something else had happened to give her some encouragement. Earlier in the book it's stated that all reality-TV talent show winners are young and pretty, including the boys, but there had, in fact, been one exception to that rule: Paul Potts — he of the interesting dentistry, who had won the first series of *Britain's Got Talent* when it aired in June 2007. Susan had seen the show and realized that despite Potts not being conventionally handsome, he'd still managed to win. An idea began to form in her mind.

'I had a bit of a rest after my mum died, but I had seen *Britain's Got Talent* on TV and thought I would have a go,' was how she summed it up. 'Paul Potts was really good. He was an inspiration to a lot of people and I thought I would take my chances.'

It was a good call, so Susan got in touch with the makers of *Britain's Got Talent* — there were rumours that, after hearing about her remarkable voice, they got in touch with her, but there doesn't appear to be any truth in the story — and began to prepare for her performance. It was a brave thing to do. Susan was aware by then that she wasn't conventionally pretty (although she had been when she was younger), and she'd had to endure Michael Barrymore clowning around and mocking her in his usual tasteless way. She'd also put up with being taunted by certain people in her village, and throughout her life she'd had to cope with the fact that many people thought she'd never amount to anything. She was also, whether she realized it or not, setting herself up for potential humiliation. The judges on *Britain's Got Talent,* Simon Cowell in particular, were not known for their gentle demeanour, and the audience could be pretty brutal, too. For a gentle, vulnerable woman like Susan, it was tantamount to entering a bear pit. But she wanted to do it for her mother all the same.

'I realized I wanted to make my mum proud of me, and the only way to do that was to take the risk and enter the show,' she said. In time-honoured fashion, Susan started rehearsing for her appearance by singing while looking in a mirror, holding a hairbrush as the microphone, 'Well, that's what everyone does,' she explained. 'I practised for a couple of weeks before the show, at least an hour a day.'

That in itself was a major breakthrough: not only was Susan singing again, she was doing so at length, fine-tuning her voice and getting it back up to scratch. Susan was reconnecting with something right at the very heart of her. Her ability to sing not only enabled her to communicate, but to prove her worth to the rest of the world.

Susan had already established something of a repertoire, including 'Memories', 'Cry Me A River' and 'Killing Me Softly', but it was with 'I Dreamed A Dream' that she decided to wow the programme makers. And what an appropriate title it was. Although the song itself deals with a woman whose illusions have been shattered, it couldn't have summed up Susan's situation better: a woman closer to fifty than forty, devastated by the loss of her mother and the failure of her many attempts to establish a singing career. Yet still she allowed herself to hope and dream, when a lesser individual would have given up years ago.

The audition for *Britain's Got Talent* was in January, although it was to be months before it hit the screens in May. Susan selected a gold dress to wear, which she had bought for a nephew's wedding — 'I bought it at a local shop,' she said — and travelled by bus to Glasgow, where she was due to perform. 'I was very nervous before I went on. I had a sandwich and then I went out there. The response from the judges really blew me away — it was a knockout. I was shocked by their reaction actually. My mouth was just wide open when they said all the nice things they did. It was the best feeling, being in front of that panel. I loved it.'

It was not, however, all plain sailing. Susan had to win her audience around, and for the first few minutes it was touch and go. 'I walked on stage and was jittery,' she told the *Daily Mail*. 'One of the questions they asked was, "What singer do you model yourself on?" A smart alec from the audience said Elvis Presley. I said, "He's dead but I'm not. Elaine Paige." There was some sniggering, but then the music came on and I just did my song. It felt bloody fantastic. I think I shocked a few people.'

Of course Susan knew what was going to happen when she opened her mouth, whereas the rest of the audience did not. If you view the clip — the most downloaded clip of 2009 — it's possible to see Susan smiling just a moment before she starts singing, and while she might have been feeling nervous, that smile is the smile of a woman who knows exactly what she's about to do. She might not have had the opportunities, but she certainly had the talent, and at long last, a lifetime of trying to get her beautiful voice noticed was about to pay off.

We've already discussed the audience's reaction to Susan's audition, but what was not clear to many people was that Susan had to wait months before the rest of the world was let in on the big secret and that, despite feeling euphoric herself, she had no one to share those feelings with. Instead she returned home alone — she'd missed the last bus, so the production company paid for a taxi — where only Pebbles was waiting to keep her company. It was an oddly anticlimactic end to one of the biggest triumphs the world of showbusiness had ever seen.

'I got home about midnight,' she told the *Daily Mail*. 'I was on such a high. It was like Celtic winning the cup. Anyway, I turned the key in the door and I walked in to silence. There was nobody to tell, so I gave my cat Pebbles a cuddle and fed her, went upstairs, hung my dress up and just went to bed. There was no big celebration. I just went home to bed. I do have the occasional glass of wine, but most of the time I'm teetotal. I prefer a half pint of lemonade.'

It's details like this that are part of Susan's enduring appeal. Unlike almost everyone else in the world of showbusiness, she is touchingly honest, with no agenda or desire to airbrush out the more painful aspects of her life and past. This little Scottish lady had just caused a sensation, and yet there she was, pottering around her house, feeding the cat and behaving as if nothing had happened. She might not even have realized it herself, of course, but Susan Boyle had just changed her life.

And so it proved five months later, when Susan's triumph was unveiled to the world. Her first inclination was to pay tribute to Bridget: 'I did it all for my late mum,' she told the *Daily Star*. 'I wanted to show her I could do something with my life. I was hoping she thought I did well. She was a woman in a million. She was unique and a lady. She taught me how to live a good life, how to behave in public and how to be a human being.' And Bridget had brought up a talented and lovely daughter, too.

Susan watched the programme with her brother John, who knew immediately that this was no ordinary talent show moment — this was something new, the likes of which had never been seen before. The world went mad.

Susan however remained modest: 'I thought there was room for improvement, particularly with the dress,' she says in her usual down-to-earth fashion. 'I love to belt out tunes in the shower because the sound is so good in the bathroom,' she told the *Sunday Mirror.* 'Music is like therapy to me. People accept me when I sing.'

It was also the first time she came to regret her remark about never having been kissed. 'Oh, I was just joking around,' she said. 'It was just banter and it has been blown out of all proportion. All I wanted to say is that I am single at the moment but I keep waiting. I am not on the hunt. I am happy as I am. It's personal.'

It should not be forgotten that while Susan might have learning difficulties, she also has her dignity, and she clearly didn't appreciate the torrent of personal opinion and speculation about her love life that poured out in the wake of that remark.

As has been mentioned earlier, Susan smartened up almost immediately after the audition — just like Paul Potts, who celebrated his triumph with some extensive dental work — and began to learn how to deal with a world that, for her, had changed overnight. There had never been a phenomenon like this before: even Paul Potts' moment of triumph had taken weeks to build up rather than happening overnight. And it could so easily not have happened at all. Susan wasn't exactly taking her life into her own hands when she sang, but it had come pretty close.

'I expected people to be a wee bit cynical,' she said. 'But I decided to win them round. That is what you do. They didn't know what to expect. Before *Britain's Got Talent,* I had never had a proper chance. It's as simple as that. You just have to keep going and take one step at a time and one day you will make it. You just don't give up.

'I knew what they were thinking. I saw people laughing and I knew they were laughing at me. But I thought, Well, they'll soon shut up when they hear me sing. And they did.'

Acres — no, forests — of newsprint were eaten up, examining the phenomenon of Susan Boyle, telling her story and attempting to analyse her appeal. There was the Cinderella aspect to it all, of course — although Cinderella was a young girl in her late teens, not a mature woman of forty-eight. Perhaps the real reason that Susan's story connected with so many and made such a lasting impact is that she represents hope and the fact that it's never too late to be what you might have been. After a genuinely difficult life, and a grief so debilitating it threatened to destroy her, Susan Boyle had triumphed over the nay sayers and doom mongers, the bullies and the school of thought that says if you're to prosper in this world you must be young and beautiful. Susan had a dream and she had dared to pursue it. It's all this that made such a formidable story, and that caused the whole world to take Susan to its heart.

And so it began. 'This is all very new to me. I went to bed one night and woke up in the morning to a group of about thirty children outside chanting my name,' she told one interviewer as she, too, struggled to understand what had happened. 'That's when it all began. John had said the night before, "Now you've seen yourself on television, so just stay in, because I think there's going to be a hell of a reaction." And, of course, there was.'

As for the makeover, in reality Susan had been pretty restrained. 'For now, I'm happy the way I am, short and plump. I wouldn't go in for Botox or anything like that,' she said.

Nor did she let it go to her head, and at the time of writing, she still hasn't. Susan had waited too long for a chance like this not to realize what she had been given, and she also knew how hard it had been to get where she now was. Inspired by her mother, she had shown every vulnerable, middle-aged person in the world that there is a future out there, and if she could do it, so could they. There was also a downside, though: the fear that she could lose it all. She later said that it was this fear that prompted the anxiety attack that led her to The Priory. For the first time in her life, Susan had something to lose.

For the time being, though, Susan took it one day at a time, chatting to reporters, inviting them into her home and talking about what an extraordinary thing it was that had happened to her. 'It has been an incredible week, but I'm just taking baby steps, seeing where it goes,' she told one. 'Singing on CBS was amazing, and being given advice and encouragement by Patti LuPone was out of this world. She's a brilliant singer. I've been very calm and relaxed. I'm taking it in my stride. I have no explanation for it, none at all. I'm just carrying on as normal. Tonight I'm staying in and having fish and chips.'

Patti LuPone no less! Susan was in a different world now, a world where different rules applied. And although those who knew and loved her and understood her frailties were concerned that the immense pressure she was under might break her, that is not the way it turned out. Susan may have had her wobbles — and they weren't over yet — but she had found an inner strength that would help her deal with everything the coming weeks and months would throw at her. She didn't crumble under the massive pressure, she didn't fall to pieces, and she did conquer Britain, as well as America, an achievement that's still very rare for a British artist.

Knowing what motivated Susan in the first place is to understand how she coped so much better than many people had forecast, and how she called upon her inner reserves to help her when the tension got too much and she came close to cracking. Susan had gone on *Britain's Got Talent* for her mother, and having had such astonishing success, she wasn't going to let her down now.

LIFE ON THE ROAD

In early June, Susan returned to Blackburn, where she received a hero's welcome. The fact that she had come second in *Britain's Got Talent* rather than first was clearly totally irrelevant. As newspaper columnists across the land were telling their readers, the dream hadn't ended, it was just beginning. Susan was reunited with her family and Pebbles, before once more removing herself from the public eye in order to continue her recovery. She wasn't staying in her own home as she clearly didn't feel up to the constant attention she received from the media and her fans.

A record deal was now firmly on the cards, as soon as Susan felt ready. Simon Cowell was keen to sign her, but he kept telling Susan the choice was hers, for there was still a feeling in some quarters that the best thing for Susan would be to return to her old life. It didn't seem to be what Susan wanted, of course, though what she would choose to do was still not totally clear.

'The best cure for her is time with her cat and her family,' he told the *News of the World,* and he was right, though behind the scenes Susan was raring to go. She had been assigned a doctor to care for her, Dr Sarah Lotzof, and the two of them had been seen out shopping together now that Susan was beginning to feel herself again. Describing her stay in The Priory as 'a little holiday', she continued, 'I want to take on the world. I've got my sleeves up ready. From now on there's nae crap.'

Susan's brother Gerry was also adamant that she was feeling much better. 'I have spoken to Susan and she is very excited and positive about the future,' he told the *News of the World.* 'She told me, "Don't worry. I'm having the time of my life." She said she felt fantastic and couldn't wait to come back home this weekend. She was giggling away and sounding more relaxed than she has in ages. That's the thing with Susan. She suffers from these mood swings, so I hope that now she's out of the clinic she's OK.'

There were still concerns, however, about whether Susan should take part in the *Britain's Got Talent* tour. While she was making a strong recovery from her anxiety attack, there was no point in pretending she wasn't still very fragile, and opinion was split as to whether she should be allowed to be part of the tour. While she was undoubtedly the biggest draw, it was made clear to Susan that she was under absolutely no obligation to take part if she didn't feel up to it. There was no point in unearthing a massive new talent if you immediately drove it into the ground, and Susan, it was becoming apparent, was a performer who needed to be treated with care.

The *Britain's Got Talent* judges continued to be quizzed about Susan's state of mind as some sectors of the public seemed to hold them responsible for what had happened to Susan. In fairness, although Simon Cowell might have had a particular obligation towards her — which he fulfilled — the other two at times seemed quite bemused by it all. Piers had appointed himself her public defender, but Amanda's role in the whole circus was more nebulous. She did, however, point out that Susan's breakdown might well have enhanced her career rather than anything else.

'You have to remember I saw Susan just three times, and can only comment on what I saw,' she told the *Daily Mail.* 'She was definitely eccentric — funny, kooky even — but there was no sign of disturbing or weird behaviour. People keep saying she has mental health issues. I still don't think she has. Yes, she struggled to cope, but anyone would. When she hit out, it was at journalists hassling her. I don't think anyone could have handled the pressure she was under. I don't think anyone — not even Piers, Simon or me — would have been able to hack it and we didn't have the sheltered background she had. At the end of the day, she was admitted to The Priory for no other reason than to have a rest. She'll be a bigger star, ironically, by coming second and by having to have a break afterwards.'

So was Susan ready for the tour? Susan herself wanted to go: she had waited so long for an opportunity that she didn't want to miss out on her big chance now that it had finally arrived. The support of Dr Lotzof was helping enormously, as soon she had 24-hour access to Susan, and so the stay in Scotland was a brief one. It wasn't long before Susan was ready to return to London, this time with Pebbles in tow, in order to prepare for the tour.

On the opening night, which took place at the Birmingham National Indoor Arena, Susan was a sensation. Before the concert began, she told fans, 'I'm feeling much better now thank you and I'm really looking forward to performing.' On stage, she was introduced by ITV2's *Britain's Got More Talent* presenter Stephen Mulhern as being 'famous all over the world. She's so famous even her cat Pebbles is famous'. Susan sang 'I Dreamed A Dream' and 'Memory' and the reception from the audience was ecstatic. If she had been in any doubt as to how much they loved her, she certainly wasn't any more.

It had been touch and go whether she'd make it on the tour. 'I honestly don't know if she'll last the full tour,' said Stephen Mulhern in an interview with *The People*. 'There are more than twenty-five dates left to go and we don't know if she'll do all of them. She arrived at the venue on time, but none of us knew whether she was going to sing. It was a case of sheer nerves for her. I was standing there with no idea what was going to happen. So I was putting together a little routine just in case. I only knew she was going to go on about twenty minutes before she did. She brought the house down. But who knows what will happen on the rest of the tour?'

There were still signs that not everything was quite right. At the second gig at the

Sheffield Arena the fans loved her as much as ever, but it was noticeable that Susan was having problems. She stumbled over the lyrics of 'Memory' — a song she knew by heart — and while she didn't appear to be suffering from stage fright, the stress seemed to be taking its toll again.

Susan managed a third concert, but at that point doctors stepped in and told her she needed to rest. The tour had begun just a week after Susan left The Priory, and while she was clearly much better, she was still exhausted as she'd had very little time to rest. In the end, and much to her chagrin, Susan was forced to pull out of the Manchester concerts.

Without underestimating what Susan was going through, all of this only added to the myth and mystery surrounding Susan. While she is as unlike a tempestuous diva as it's possible to be, this was classic diva behaviour — leaving it till the last second before deciding if they're going to show up, then cancelling their concerts at the last minute. And although the reasons for Susan's behaviour were very different, the 'will she, won't she' game not only continued to keep her in the headlines, but underlined her fragility, which in many ways was part of her appeal. Susan was, after all, the woman who had battled her demons to get to where she was today, and the fact that her battle had been such a public one was doing her no harm at all.

Now the tour was reaching Susan's native Scotland, the big question on everyone's lips was, would she be able to perform on the Glasgow stage? The answer was an emphatic yes, not least because this is where Susan had sung the first audition, the one that had turned her into a star. The 9,000-strong audience gave her a standing ovation before she'd even sung a note, and this time she was word perfect. These were her people and she wasn't going to let them down.

The contrast in her appearance this time round was more marked than ever before. Sleek, coiffed and wearing a shimmery grey dress, when Susan made it on to the stage, she looked as if she was born to be there. Her evident delight in performing, and her happiness in front of the audience, towards whom she blew kisses, was there for all to see. The hip wiggling had gone, too, having been replaced by the kind of bow you'd expect from a veteran performer. It seemed hard to imagine that her first performance had gone global less than two months earlier, and that this amazing transformation had been achieved so quickly. A star had truly been born.

As the tour progressed, Simon Cowell appeared on *GMTV,* ostensibly to talk about another of his vehicles, *The X Factor.* Inevitably, though, he wasn't able to dodge the subject of his most famous protégé. He was quite open about the pressures on Susan, and even admitted that he would have been prepared for it had she decided not to enter the final of the show.

'Everyone is writing about her, she's in the spotlight and she found it difficult to cope with that, and at that point even I sat down with her and said, "Look, if this is getting too much for you, you don't have to go into the final, no one is going to force you",' he said. 'You do whatever you want, no one is going to force you. And she looked me in the eye and said, "No, I want to win this competition, I want to give it a go," and that was the decision we all made, and I thought that she wanted to do it, but it was only at the moment that she lost that it hits you and you go, "How is she going to cope with this?" And she found it very, very difficult. You can't predict how things are going to escalate and how well that person can cope. What I don't want to do at the beginning is go through a whole kind of psychological evaluation because I think, for me, that is almost discrimination.'

As far as the concerts were concerned, and the missed gig in Manchester, Simon had been as much in the dark about her actions as anyone else. 'I genuinely didn't know what she was going to do,' he said. Our feeling was that there are ten or twelve acts on the bill, but that everyone, like me, said, "We don't want to force her into performing but hopefully you'll enjoy the show" — it's a tricky one.'

Susan now had her own spokeswoman, and she explained that all that had been amiss in Manchester was that she needed a rest. There's no doubt that 'rest' was a big issue: performers need stamina when they go on tour and Susan, for obvious reasons, had never done anything like it before. In order to capitalize on audience interest in the participants, the tour crams as many dates as possible into as short a space of time as possible — without wishing to sound unduly cynical, there was a good chance the ticket-buying public would have forgotten who most of the acts were had the organizers waited too long — which meant that people like Susan, who had only ever performed in a very modest way, had to adapt to the demands of a strenuous agenda. While Susan might have been tired, there was no sign at all of any form of mental collapse. For Susan, it had finally begun to sink in that her dream was coming true.

Susan was clearly determined to give the fans in her homeland a treat. After Glasgow, the tour moved on to Edinburgh, where Susan again provoked scenes of near hysteria and adulation when she appeared onstage. Meanwhile, it was confirmed that she had signed a record deal with Cowell, to be produced under his Syco label, and even then it was clear that it was going to be a massive bestseller.

The tour promoters were taking no chances with Susan, treating her as gently as they could. While the other acts were ferried round the country in a tour bus, Susan got her own limo. She was also finally getting used to dealing with her fans. Although she frequently appeared tired as she moved between gigs, she always waved at the crowds, signed autographs when she could and greeted the people who had gathered to see her. The small public backlash that had begun just before the final seemed to have completely disappeared. Now that people knew she was battling on, Susan inspired only respect and affection — and a huge amount of it — wherever she went.

Unfortunately, Susan was not able to perform at the next date in Cardiff. But while there were reports in the press that she had missed half the dates on the tour, the more realistic way of looking at it was that she had managed to appear in half of them. Life on the road is so utterly at odds with everything Susan was used to that it's a minor miracle she had adapted as well as she had. Private limos, five-star hotels, screaming fans and euphoric audiences were not something Susan had ever experienced before, and while the same could be said of the other participants on the tour, they didn't have Susan's unique circumstances. All things considered, she was coping remarkably well.

All the while, Simon Cowell was keeping a very close eye on the proceedings. For starters, he had a vested financial interest in Susan, who was now signed to his record label, and if she turned out to have a long-term career, he stood to benefit quite as much as she did. Then there was the moral aspect as well. If there was one person responsible for the huge change in Susan's circumstances, it was Cowell, and he felt a duty of care towards her, too.

In the wake of all the fuss about whether

or not she would appear on stage during the tour, Cowell confessed that there had been some mistakes, particularly when it came to the hype built up around Susan and the fact that she didn't actually win. It is difficult to see what else he could have done, however — the Boyle phenomenon was an entirely spontaneous global event and not a carefully manufactured Cowell extravaganza — but Susan could, perhaps, have been given more support.

'During the final show, at the crucial point when the dance group Diversity won, I looked over at her face and thought, "Christ, she doesn't know how to deal with not winning",' Cowell wrote in the *Sunday Mirror.* 'It was a bad moment. Afterwards, I went over and gave her a hug and tried to reassure her. 'Susan,' I said, 'my offer to record an album with you still stands.' And we agreed that we would work together; that it wasn't the end of the road for her. After that, I left the studio. I remember having a drink that night and trying to relax, but still feeling a bit strange. Something just didn't feel right. And sure enough, it wasn't.' As her stay in The Priory proved.

Cowell was perfectly honest about the issues Susan's appearance had provoked: should people who might be a little fragile be allowed to appear on the show? Fame is a very strange beast and will often savage the person it initially befriends, but the point that Simon and Piers both made was that for all the difficulties Susan endured, the positives far outweighed the negatives. She had, after all, achieved her lifelong dream.

Cowell discussed this with Susan's family. 'Last week, I met them in my London office and I asked them, "Tell me honestly, did we do right or did we do wrong?" ' he related. 'What I meant was, was it right to allow Susan to carry on performing in the show once it became clear that she was finding it stressful? And they said, unanimously, that we did the right thing. They said that Susan has always wanted to sing and had sat at home for years, wishing that she had a chance. We had given her that opportunity.'

Susan was now receiving the care she needed, though it was an issue that was unlikely to go away. In an episode totally unrelated to Susan, a contestant on *The X Factor,* a woman in her fifties, publicly claimed she was going to commit suicide after not getting through to the final, which gave rise to more fears about what happened when you put people unused to fame in the spotlight. A lot of the time, it turns out they just can't cope.

Whatever had happened in the past, Susan was doing well now. There was still some comment in the press to the effect that she shouldn't be on the tour, but the fact was that Susan very much wanted to be there, and the only thing that was distressing her was when she wasn't able to appear. She missed another show in Nottingham, but was due on stage at Wembley, where she was determined to perform.

'Susan gets really upset because she thinks she's letting her fans down,' said her spokeswoman. 'But she's got to balance making her fans happy with looking after her health. She would have loved to have been at the shows, but she's just really tired. She's in London resting now, but she's feeling really positive and can't wait to get back on stage. She's really excited about Sunday's show — she loves singing . . . she lives for singing. If she were told she couldn't perform at all because she had to take a break it would break her heart. And she still has a lot of support from her fans — she gets a standing ovation every time she sings and it means so much to her.'

Susan duly sang at the two Wembley dates and remained adamant that she was loving every second and simply wanted the dream to go on. Now there was more than just the tour to worry about, though: now that she had signed a record deal with Cowell, there were tracks to pick and music to record. And so the process began, with Simon professing to love what they were turning out. 'She sounds fantastic on record,' he said, refusing to give any more specific details about what they would be releasing. 'It's not all going to be show tunes. It's not an obvious record, but so far, it's good. She's got a really good recording voice and I'm going to take my time. She's happy and I think she's enjoying the process. Luckily, things have quietened down a bit.'

They had indeed to a certain extent. The world seemed to have got over the difference in Susan's appearance and voice — though if truth be told, she now bore no resemblance to the lady who'd first auditioned — but remained utterly fascinated by her strange and poignant story. Plans were afoot to run organized tours of Blackburn, although in truth there's little that stands out there apart from Susan. The demand was there, though, especially from the United States, which remained transfixed by everything to do with Susan Boyle. The Americans were not alone. In June,

the French-born, Glasgow-based artist Laetitia Guilbaud, caused uproar when she
painted a portrait of Susan that made her
look like something out of the Folies
Bergère. In the portrait, Susan's waist is
cinched in by a corset, while a very low-cut
top shows off a deep décolletage (something
the real Susan would never wear, having
always dressed extremely modestly). She is
also smoking a cigar, while one gloved hand
clutches a satin purse and another strokes
the pearls at her neck. There is the tattoo of
an 'S' on her thigh, while beside her sits an
ice bucket filled with champagne.

It was certainly a novel take on Susan.
'For me, even though she is not the most
attractive lady in the world, she has come
into the spotlight recently with her beautiful
voice and singing talent,' Guilbaud explained. 'I felt obliged to paint her in my
style and give her a bit of "je ne sais quoi"
and make her more sexy and appealing in a
physical way to go with her voice and also
wanted to reveal a wild side to her now that
she is a celebrity.'

The pictures were pretty innocuous, all
told: no one had depicted Susan as a sauce-
pot before, and there was certainly nothing
gratuitous or cruel intended by it. But some
of Susan's fans, especially those who lived

in the United States, were unhappy with the portrayal of their heroine. Susan appealed to a wide variety of people, but one particular section of society who liked her were the very religious, and they were incensed by Guilbaud's portrait to the extent that they issued threats. An email campaign was begun, orchestrated by a fundamentalist Christian group based in Texas. A typical email read, 'This work is a mean depiction of a precious child of God. The artist should be crucified.' While another said, 'Susan is an angel. She would never behave in this way. Guilbaud should look to God and pray there is no retribution.'

Laetitia was extremely taken aback. 'My artwork was never intended to insult or be hurtful,' she said. 'I am a fan of Susan. When I read the first few emails I was very scared. Some of them were threatening me. In one week I got thousands of blog hits and emails. About 200 were sick. They came from Texas.' In the event, not everyone was so squeamish: the picture was displayed in Glasgow's ArtDeCaf gallery and remains prominent on Laetitia's website.

All of these were examples of Susan's astonishing reach, and as well as touching people's hearts all over the globe, she showered people with her gold dust by association. *Britain's Got Talent* judge Amanda's career continued to go from strength to strength in the United States, which she cheerfully admitted was entirely due to the Susan Boyle effect. She was interviewed so many times about Boyle that American TV companies continued to use her on other projects. And heaven help anyone who made nasty remarks about Susan: when Sharon Osbourne spewed out something unpleasant about her, she was forced into a humiliating climb-down and apology soon after. The world didn't want to hear this sort of nastiness. Susan was a fragile creature with a huge amount of talent and people felt highly protective of her, even if, in some cases, they took it a little far.

Paul Potts continued to watch Susan's progress with interest, too. Both artists were aware of the comparisons made between them, and it seemed to make good commercial sense for them to collaborate at some time. But even Potts blanched at the kind of attention Susan was receiving, which went well beyond anything he'd had to deal with. 'She's done really well and she's coped with the sudden media attention,' he said. 'I don't know how I would have coped.' Potts said he was hoping to sing a duet with

Susan at some point in the future, but said it was too early to think about that yet. 'I wouldn't want to add any more pressure than she has already,' he explained. 'It is obvious she is finding it tough and I hope that she will be left alone.'

Susan didn't appear to mind, though. She might have found the pressure tough, but the idea of having it all taken away from her was a lot tougher.

Meanwhile, the revamp continued. In July Susan flew to the United States to appear on the *Today Show,* forcing Barack Obama to switch his TV health care address to the nation because it would have clashed with the interview. By now Susan looked even trimmer. Her haircut was slicker, her make-up more polished, and she appeared to have lost some weight, clad as she was in an elegant purple dress. The show's host, Meredith Vieira, asked her if she'd had a makeover.

'Just a slight one,' said Susan, looking coy. 'I brush up quite well.'

Susan also spoke about the bullying she'd endured as a child. 'It wasn't easy for me as a little kid, no, because I got ridiculed in school,' she said. 'You always get that from your peers anyway. I'm the type of person that just couldn't stand up for herself very well, but I got over it. I'm getting over it now.'

And how did she find being so famous? Vieira asked. 'I'm having a great time,' said Susan firmly. 'It's been unbelievable. It's indescribable. Anyone who has that kind of impact finds it hard to get their head around it. The impact [was] like a demolition ball . . . I've got to be honest here, through the guidance of a great team, and they are very good, I was able to see that in perspective and really turn that around a little. Being plucked from obscurity is like going on a long journey. You never know how it's going to end. I don't want it to end.'

That should have been enough to silence the doubters, but it wasn't. They felt that Susan would have been better off returning to obscurity in Blackburn, but it was plain that Susan disagreed. Increasingly these people acted as if they knew what was best for Susan, and some people continued to fulminate that she was unable to cope. All the while Susan was jetting back and forth across the Atlantic, looking more and more polished with each journey. What the doubters didn't realize, of course, was that they were treating Susan in exactly the same way the rest of the world had always treated her

— until she showed she had a talent. Susan had spent her entire adult life being told that others knew what was best for her, and this was the first time she was having any say herself. It was a turnaround she appeared to be relishing.

At any rate, anyone who had the kind of clout that forced the President of the United States into rescheduling wasn't going to go away in a hurry. As well as revealing the full extent of the impact Susan had made, that episode of the *Today Show* featured Elaine Paige, who Susan had so famously said she wanted to emulate. Susan was stunned when her idol came on, telling the audience she was 'absolutely gobsmacked'. Then there was a specially filmed clip of Donny Osmond, pointing to a poster of himself and Marie in his Las Vegas show: Susan should come and see the show, he said, and possibly replace Marie.

Not only was Susan's newfound fame beginning to sink in, she was also beginning to see the financial rewards of all her hard work. Her home in Blackburn belonged to the council, and now she began to make plans to buy it. She was also learning how to use a mobile phone for the first time, although her brother Gerry asserted she hadn't quite got the hang of texting. Susan now had a credit card, a PA, a bodyguard (which she needed — those crowds could get boisterous) and most importantly of all, Simon Cowell's secret mobile number, the one he almost never gives out.

Cowell was taking his responsibilities seriously: there had been one near breakdown and he wasn't taking any chances of it happening again. Meanwhile, Susan, who was about to start work on her album, was being housed in a spacious, minimalist flat in Kensington, a very upmarket area of London, where Pebbles was also holding court. Was she ever going to go back to Scotland? Well, yes, of course she was, but she was certainly experiencing a very different world to the one she was used to.

Susan really hit the big time when she was asked to pose for the September cover of the US magazine *Harper's Bazaar.* It was an incredibly prestigious gig as the magazine, an upmarket glossy, was associated with high-end sophistication and its covers are usually filled with extremely beautiful women. Susan was entering a different league. 'It really made me feel like a Hollywood actress,' she confided. 'I had my hair done up.' She certainly looked extremely glamorous, even more than she had previously.

The only downside as far as Susan was concerned was the fear that everything would be whipped away again. Showbusiness is a notoriously fickle industry, and no one's career is guaranteed, but at least she was in the right hands. 'Susan absolutely loves the life she is leading now,' her brother Gerry said in an interview with the *Sunday Mirror.* 'But it has left her fearful of going back to how things were, living on her own and waiting for her singing dream to come true. She has asked me many times what happens if this all stops?' There was no answer to that, although at least Susan would be a lot better off than she had been previously.

Gerry also appreciated what Cowell was doing for his sister. 'Simon called me to a meeting and was very determined to let me know, as her brother, that she will be managed delicately,' he said. 'I saw a different side to him. His TV persona is one thing. But he made it clear to me he has Susan's best interests at heart. As a family we needed to hear that.' He was certainly doing everything in his power to make her life as comfortable as it could be. But there was much more to come. *Harper's Bazaar* was due out shortly — and there was a record launch to plan.

GLAMMING UP

When the *Harper's Bazaar* featuring Susan appeared, it caused a sensation. Susan was looking better and better by now: there were clear signs of weight loss now, and the way she had been styled made her appear positively soignée. She was dressed beautifully, too, in an array of designer outfits that it would have been inconceivable for her to have worn previously. In one shot she sports a sequinned Donna Karan top that, for the first time ever, showed a hint of cleavage. She was still demonstrably Susan, just a glossier version, and had managed the transformation without destroying the essence of what it was to be her.

Susan was clearly loving every minute of her newfound fame. The photo session had taken place at the country house hotel Clivedon in Buckinghamshire, which had been the setting for another un-Susan-like episode decades earlier: the parties at the centre of the Profumo scandal. The pictures of Susan in her new glamorous incarnation capture her sitting at a piano in a long, black, Tadashi Shoji taffeta gown, while others show her relaxing in brightly coloured dresses and coats, a world away from her former rather drab garb. Most notable, however, is how happy and relaxed Susan looks in the pictures. The days when she appeared to be struggling with how much her life had changed seemed well and truly in the past.

Susan had always considered it to be her destiny to be a singer, and now, at long last, she was being proved right. But having established her vocal talent, she had to look the part, and if that meant a wardrobe full of designer clothing, so be it. Susan might not be interested in her appearance, but she was well aware that others were, on top of which she had been rather dismayed by the early photographs that were taken of her. In the end she was only too happy to go along with the makeover, putting herself in the safe hands of this upmarket fashion magazine.

So spectacular was her transformation that the woman behind it — Laura Brown, *Harper's* special projects manager — was interviewed about it on NBC's *Today Show*.

'The idea behind the shoot was a very, very simple one,' she said. 'It was to take gorgeous, glamorous and sensitive portraits of her. This was her first magazine photo shoot, so you can't do too much too soon.' But what they had done was spectacular. Now you could see the pretty young woman that Susan once had been.

Laura had been as swept away by Susan's story as everyone else. Rarely can a duckling have turned so rapidly into a swan, and it all started that night, in front of a television audience of millions, a moment that was to change Susan's life.

'She came on to the stage and just transfixed us all,' Laura continued. 'She's become a hero to a lot of people with dreams of stardom, or who maybe have a talent but have been too scared to express it. And I think everyone's heart soared when they saw her sing that day. I think Susan is getting more and more used to being in the spotlight and being on television and being photographed. Since April, you've seen her look just day to day become more polished and refined. And she's growing in her confidence with what she'll wear and how she'll be perceived.'

Something else that was changing was that Susan was beginning to have more fun —

something that had been sorely missing from her life to date. Now finally she seemed to be enjoying herself, relaxing and going with the moment. 'She actually did a little bit of moonwalking in her Giuseppe Zanotti heels at one point,' said Laura. 'What we did on our shoot was give her a little bit of a haircut, and that was it, and a little bit of a curl. And actually the shape of her hair is great. She's got a really lovely curl to it. So we just tidied it up a little bit and paired it with some natural make-up, and she looked great.' It was something of an understatement as the transformation was phenomenal.

Susan's interview with *Harper's* was pretty revealing, too. For a short time, Susan appeared to be thinking of leaving Scotland for good, given that she'd been living in London for some months now. 'I'll go back to visit, but you have to move on,' she said. As for her newfound fame, she commented, 'It will take a bit of adjusting to, because I've led a sheltered life. I've got life experience, but mentally I have to adjust. But it's all good, it's all good.' And then, really unexpectedly, she revealed she was a fan of Madonna: 'I like that she is a diverse pop star and controversial,' she said.

Indeed, Susan's tastes were turning out to

be considerably more catholic with a small 'c' than anyone could have imagined. She'd already covered a Rolling Stones number and now she was praising Madonna. There was clearly more to Susan than met the eye. But it only served to illustrate what Susan had always been up against: being judged by her appearance and assumed to be a lesser person and a lesser talent than she was. Now that she'd been given her chance, she continued to amaze and surprise.

The *Harper's Bazaar* pictures caused a sensation and proved that interest in Susan showed no sign of abating. Piers Morgan, who was in the States at that time, related that he had just met the actor Robin Williams, who only seemed to want to talk about Susan Boyle. There continued to be talk of a film based on Susan's life, with Catherine Zeta-Jones' name cropping up to play the lead role.

Meanwhile, Diversity, the band that had won *Britain's Got Talent,* were forced to deny that there was any rift with Simon Cowell over Susan's seemingly preferential treatment. There had been reports in the press that there were tensions, as Cowell appeared to be concentrating on Susan's career rather than theirs. Certainly, there was no contest as to who had the higher profile. Diversity themselves were full of plans for the future, happily talking about being seen as role models for a younger generation, and wisely heaping praise on Susan. But despite their undoubted talent, they didn't have Susan's back story, and they hadn't captured the public's imagination in quite the same way.

There had been predictions in the early days that interest in Susan would be short lived, but in reality nothing could be further from the truth. The whole world seemed to want a piece of Susan. Lord Glasgow, the chief of the Clan Boyle, extended an invitation to Susan to attend the next clan gathering, while it emerged that the famous chemist Robert Boyle and the film director Danny Boyle — of *Slum-dog Millionaire* fame — were both distant relations. Hollywood continued to be utterly fascinated by her, as did the rest of the world.

Elaine Paige, with whom it seemed increasingly likely that Susan would perform a duet, had her say, too, claiming that Cowell had stopped her from warning Susan in advance what fame was really like. She had, of course, commented on Susan previously, before going on to meet her, but she now felt she should have been allowed to give Susan a little advice. 'Nothing prepares you for the overwhelming fame and the media interest in your life,' she said. 'I wanted to warn her of what was to come, but he [Cowell] wouldn't allow that. Instead, I surprised her when she was on the *Today Show* in America. She still seemed overwhelmed by things when we met, but hopefully we will get the chance to sing together.'

The fact that Susan had been so overwhelmed and had suffered from some well-documented difficulties relating to her overnight success had wider-reaching effects too, changing the modus operandi of reality TV. There had been real public anger about what some had seen as Susan's exploitation, and the television community needed to address that fact if they wanted to regain the public's trust and approval. It should be noted that Susan herself didn't share these concerns or anger: she was well aware of the positive differences that *Britain's Got Talent* had made to her life.

There was also going to be more attention paid from now on to the age of the contestants who appeared on these types of shows. Cowell had come under repeated criticism for making small children cry on stage, although in fairness a great deal of the responsibility should lie with their parents. If they were concerned and felt their children couldn't take the criticism, they should never have allowed them on stage.

A new series of *The X Factor* was due to begin in August, and for the first time, in a bow to public concerns, it was to include some form of psychological appraisal for the contestants. They were also going to be offered more support if they found it difficult to cope with the pressure and the attention they received. No one wanted a repeat of Susan's episode in The Priory, although it seemed a little unfair that Susan, who was now coping remarkably well, was always the first to be mentioned when the subject of reality TV stars going to pieces was raised.

Susan's full-time assistant, Ciaran Doig, was certainly helping her to cope. The two of them paid a quiet visit to Blackburn, where Susan was pictured attending church, and stayed in her old family home — London might have had the bright lights, but home was, after all, home. There were other, more subtle changes in the way Susan was perceived in the community. Once back in her old neighbourhood she was asked for her autograph, another acknowledgement of her new status. There was no sign of the people who had made her life difficult in the past — no doubt they felt nothing but shame for the way they'd behaved — and if they had tried to do anything to upset this national treasure, they would most probably have been lynched.

Susan was such hot property by now that she regularly cropped up in debates about the television industry. The nature of reality TV was under constant scrutiny: there had been at least two reality TV–related suicides in recent years — one in the UK and one in the States — and there was a lot of concern about the ethics of the genre. In the UK, the tragedy had occurred in the wake of an episode of *Wife Swap.* One participating couple had been honest about the fact that they had an open marriage and had indulged in affairs with other people. In the wake of the show the husband, Simon Foster, lost his job, the marriage broke down and his life fell apart, and he subsequently committed suicide. In the States, meanwhile, a contestant on *American Idol,* Paula Goodspeed, committed suicide close to the home of one of the judges, Paula Abdul. Both cases were more extreme than Susan's, but they did highlight many of the same issues and concerns, especially those relating to mental health.

The big question, though, was whether or not an appearance on a reality television show could lead to a new and lasting career? The answer appeared to be yes when you consider examples like Paul Potts and Will Young. But the annals of reality television are also littered with the corpses of those who made an initial breakthrough but failed to go any further, in many cases becoming extremely bitter about their experience. Was it possible that Susan could become one of those?

Louis Walsh, the man behind Westlife and Boyzone and one of Cowell's fellow judges on *The X Factor*, had followed the debate with interest. Her case was so unusual, the pressures on her so unique and the issues surrounding her so delicate that it was unknown territory.

'I think she could have a massive record, but I don't know if she is able, due to all the pressure that she will be under,' he said in a speech to the Edinburgh International Television Festival. 'I'd get a very good tour manager on the road with Susan to make sure that he lets her work as little as possible. I'd get her to bed early at night and give her sleeping tablets. That's the answer. There will be an awful lot of pressure on her, but once the record is out there and they make the right video for her she will be fine.'

Ant and Dec were also at the festival and were keen to defend the decision to allow Susan to take part in the show. Their views are worth listening to because both of them were child stars, meeting on the set of children's programme *Byker Grove,* and both had had extensive experience of reality television in all its formats, as well as being the hosts of *I'm A Celebrity . . . Get Me Out Of Here!* and *Britain's Got Talent.* Both had seen at first hand what reality television can do to a person and both, rightly, felt that it would have been grossly unfair to deny Susan, and others like her, a chance.

'You can't start censoring people because you don't think they would be able to handle the fame and the attention as well as they should,' said Ant, reminding the audience that he himself had been only eleven when he'd started his TV career. 'You can't turn round and say you don't think she's going to handle it that well so we won't have her on the show.' There was also the fact that, despite a wobbly start, Susan was definitely learning how to handle it. Given the right amount of help, she seemed perfectly able to cope.

'People don't turn up with it written on T-shirts how sane they are,' added Dec. 'You can't tell by looking at somebody. Susan was a single woman who lives in a small town in Scotland and came along to fulfill a dream. How do you stand there and say, "You can't go on, we're not sure you'll be able to handle it?" You can't do that.'

It should be noted that while Susan may have had mild learning difficulties, there was never any suggestion that she was in any way mentally ill. Her brothers had been keen to make that clear, but despite their insistence, it's a misconception that has lingered in the public consciousness. Finding it difficult to cope with overnight global fame, especially when you've led a sheltered life, is simply not the same as being mentally ill.

Ant and Dec were right: everyone deserves a chance. Susan would certainly have agreed with them, because she was loving every minute of her glory, clocking up one triumph after another. At the end of August her CD, *I Dreamed A Dream,* was posted on Amazon for pre-ordering, and despite the fact that it wouldn't be released for another three months, it shot straight to number one.

There was some curiosity about the tracks chosen to go on the CD, especially a cover of Madonna's 'You'll See', which explained Susan's recent enthusiasm for the artist in

Harper's Bazaar. 'Susan chose it herself — it's a song she has loved for years,' a friend who wished to remain nameless told the *Sun.* 'She sang it at auditions for TV shows and music contests when she used to be cruelly turned away by people. At the end, when she was sometimes reduced to tears, she used to say, "You'll see". And she's proof she can do it now as one of the most famous women in the world.'

A picture was released from the album's shoot, showing a smiling and relaxed Susan in the beautiful Scottish countryside, against a backdrop of the mountains of the Ardkinglas Estate in Cairndow, Argyll. Meanwhile, there were more firsts: she was spotted buying designer clothes in Harrods, a shop she had never visited before, while Pebbles got a session in a pet pampering salon.

Susan's personal style had noticeably changed, but she didn't swan around in the kind of clothes she'd worn for the *Harper's* shoot on a day-to-day basis. The magazine had simply proved that she could look attractive in the style of the modern woman, and as a result she took more pains with her appearance than she had done before. Her brothers had already commented on the fact that Susan used to be extremely careless about her looks, and that they'd often chided her for not running a comb through her hair. But it would seem that there was something self-defensive about her actions. If Susan was convinced she was ugly, then it was safer to play up to that perception than try to do something about it and risk exposing herself to ridicule.

But Susan was not ugly; far from it. She had simply allowed herself to become unkempt and when, with the help of others, she woke up to the fact that she could look as good as anyone, she seized the chance. This is another often overlooked upside of reality television: it allows people to explore a completely different side of themselves and their lives.

As the Boyle phenomenon continued to grow, other female stars mused on what lay ahead for Susan. Elaine Paige had already said she wanted to warn Susan of the potential perils afoot, and to her great credit she had shown nothing but warmth and generosity to Susan since that first audition, which now seemed like a lifetime ago. Now it was the turn of another star, a fellow Scottish singer, Lulu. Lulu and a great many other seasoned performers were as stunned as the public by the world's reaction to Susan, not least because it was so different from how they had made their names. But even if her route to success had been different, Lulu, too, had experienced sudden fame, and as such knew what the downsides could be.

'It is hard to say if Susan Boyle mania is justified,' she told the *Daily Record* a little tactlessly. 'It's amazing. It steps over into celebrity and that is hard to deal with. In a way, it would be better to just let her sing her song and go home. But you have to take both. I just hope she is going to be able to handle it because it's not easy. Everyone can trip up and have their hiccups, but it's about how you recover.'

Susan had already had her hiccup, and appeared to be recovering beautifully, so it was unrealistic to expect her to just go home after the event. Other, more seasoned stars would probably have been a little bewildered by it all, but the fact was that the phenomenon had happened and Susan wasn't going to go away. What was important, though, as Lulu acknowledged, was that she had proper guidance and management, for without that she really would encounter problems.

'When I found fame, it was very exciting and scary at the same time,' Lulu continued. 'I was carried off in a whirlwind. I had a very nice manager who was a mother figure, so I was fortunate. It's hard to do the work if you don't have the right people around you.' The right support was something Susan did have — Simon had made sure of that.

Lulu also made the point that in this day and age, Susan would have had a lot of trouble breaking into the music industry on her own, because today's stars are expected not only to be young and beautiful, but to cavort about wearing almost nothing. Lulu's strict father would never have allowed her to do that, she said, but that only served to emphasize another aspect of Susan's story. The idea of Susan cavorting about the place half dressed was unthinkable, which meant she was one of the few modern-day stars who knew for a fact they had made it on the basis of talent — and a good back story — alone. No one doubts that Girls Aloud are an entertaining bunch of singers, but it hasn't hurt that they are toothsome as well.

Lulu's comments, while well-intentioned, missed an important point. Despite the fact that she was being hauled into practically every debate about reality television, it was difficult to draw general conclusions, because Susan's story is unique. Yes, she clearly needed the right people around her to guide her career, and yes, the sudden leap into the limelight must have been extremely difficult, but what could really be said about Susan was this: nothing like this had ever happened to anybody else before.

According to the man himself, she'd made Cowell get in touch with his inner, caring side. Over in the States, Amanda was interviewing Simon on CBS's *The Early Show,* as a new series of *America's Got Talent* was about to begin. He was very frank about the way that Susan had changed his attitude, not just towards her, but towards all reality television stars. 'I think at the point where she didn't win, she was afraid everything would be taken away from her and she was going to go back to that little house. She didn't want to go back to that life,' he said, adding that he now felt far more responsible towards other people who came on his shows. 'We're used to it [fame]; they're not. [But] After all the dust settled, she was happy. She is stunning on record. She's going to sell millions of records this year.' Indeed, he continued, Susan had been so delighted when she heard the results of the recording that she'd actually burst into tears.

Given the Cowell connection, it was no surprise when it was announced that Susan was going to sing on *America's Got Talent,* in her first live performance outside the UK. 'NBC are buzzing with excitement about Miss Boyle's performance,' said a member of the production company. 'All the networks have been putting in requests for her to appear on their shows, but it seemed fitting that she should make her US TV singing début on *America's Got Talent.*' Indeed, she could scarcely have chosen a more appropriate show. And so, in early September, Susan jetted off to LA, the celebrity capital of the world, where she got a first-hand glimpse of how much the United States loved her.

There was a massive crowd waiting for her at the airport, chanting her name and crying, 'We love you, Susan.' The crowd was held back, but one little fan managed to break through and give her a hug. Susan initially looked as if she could scarcely take in the reaction, but she soon recovered, beaming at the crowd, blowing them kisses and waving, before she was escorted into a waiting limousine. 'I was delighted to be given such a warm welcome,' she said afterwards. 'It was really lovely for so many people to meet me. I'm totally overwhelmed.'

Once in LA, she was treated like the A-lister she'd become. Nothing was too much trouble. Susan and her newly acquired retinue were taken on a visit to Disneyland in Anaheim, California, where they were pictured enjoying the rides. Susan had a number of minders with her now, which was very necessary considering the fact that she was even more popular in the States than she was in the UK, and was regularly mobbed wherever she went.

Back in the UK, the debate raged as to whether or not Susan had been exploited, despite the fact that she was very publicly loving every minute of her new life. The latest person to wade into the debate — and there was no shortage of people prepared to do so — was Jean Rogers, the vice president of Equity, the actors' union, who claimed that reality TV shows were nothing more than freak shows. 'Susan Boyle was catapulted into fame by *Britain's Got Talent,*' she said, 'which is the modern equivalent of the Victorian freak show. The truth is that Susan Boyle is a vulnerable and exploited middle-aged woman. Her fairytale did come true, but at a high physical and mental cost. This is not an excuse to get at Simon Cowell or anyone else who survived their apprenticeships and deserves their success. It's about fairness. Everyone gets paid — everyone except the performers. The performers are workers in a highly competitive and exploitative industry where their hopes and dreams are manipulated. Britain has got talent . . . so let's pay them.'

Rogers seems to have completely and fundamentally misunderstood the role of reality television and the contestants on the show. Susan Boyle — the 'vulnerable and exploited middle-aged woman' — was now an international star, and as we've often repeated in this book, she had no desire to go back to her old life. She'd spent decades trying to fight her way out of it, and having been presented with the opportunity of a lifetime, she had seized it with both hands. As for paying the contestants, well that was what they were: contestants. No one was forcing them to enter the competition and the rewards, if they did manage to win or get noticed, were very great indeed.

Back in LA, the last thing Susan would have wanted was for the likes of Jean Rogers to stop her appearing on the television screen. Her performance on *America's Got Talent,* which was watched by 25 million viewers, was an absolute triumph. She performed 'I Dreamed A Dream', as well as 'Wild Horses' — the first time she had sung the number in public. It was later released as a single and went some way towards addressing the critics who had complained that she only ever sang two songs, 'I Dreamed A Dream' and 'Memory' — she was clearly capable of a great deal more. Susan looked the part, as well: she was clad in an elegant black gown and sang in front of a full orchestra. Unsurprisingly, she got a standing ovation.

Many of the reviews for her appearance pointed out what an outstanding performer she'd become. 'Watch out Mariah [Carey], there's a new diva in town!' wrote one critic, while the *Los Angeles Times* said, 'Time to take Susan seriously. She should no longer be considered a sideshow. She should be appreciated for her singing ability.' 'She wasn't even a competitor, but Susan Boyle arguably stole the finale of *America's Got Talent,*' added The Huffington Post, while the website E! Online agreed: 'Who won *America's Got Talent*? Besides Susan Boyle, that is.'

Piers Morgan was there to witness Susan's latest triumph. By now she was becoming something of an established showbiz hand, and was able to have a chat with him behind the scenes. Susan was certainly living the lifestyle, too. She was staying at the swanky Hotel Bel Air, and was seen on a shopping trip to upmarket department store Barneys, a favourite with the *Sex And The City* girls. It helped that Cowell was in town and was a part of it all: Susan had come to rely on him and to trust him, too.

Susan's brother Gerry also seemed happier about the way things were going. 'She is in a great place right now and very confident about her career at this point as her new album apparently sounds excellent,' he said. 'This is a totally different set of circumstances [from before] and Susan is totally more relaxed. She's in a great place. Simon Cowell is going to meet with her in America and he has assured us that he will do everything he can to protect Susan and to promote her in the correct fashion. I know Simon has a surly reputation, but I think he is a very trustworthy person who has my sister's best interests at heart.'

Susan had another triumphant return to Britain. She was feeling so much better now that she was able to talk about the strain she'd been under and even about her stay in The Priory. 'With no pressure and then suddenly having all this pressure I found it suffocating,' she told the *Daily Record*. 'I don't remember much after the final. All I do remember is being put in an ambulance and taken to a clinic. I was tired. I look back now and it was a necessity because I was so

tired. I used to be a kind of spectator looking outward at the world. Now I am part of
that world. I am not frightened, I am going
to embrace it because I feel a bit more
confident in myself. I am more able to cope,
more able to take part in the dream. I'm
ready to get there and get on with it now. I
am not the wee frightened lassie I used to
be.'

Could there have been any more vigorous
proof that Susan's life had been totally
transformed by reality TV? There was
frenzied speculation in the press that Susan
would end up bigger than the Beatles, not
least because she'd cracked the notoriously
difficult American market with no effort at
all.

Meanwhile, back in the UK Susan was
being pitched head first against none other
than Robbie Williams in the race for the
number one slot in the Christmas album
charts. Ironically, Robbie had spent years
trying and failing to crack the American
market — something Susan had done with
ease — and it was another indication of how
far she had come that she was being tipped
to win the race.

'No contest. It is Susan Boyle,' said the
veteran music industry commentator Paul
Gambaccini. 'That is not an insult to Rob-

bie Williams, it is just that, bizarre as it sounds, Boyle is the new-artist story of the year around the world. The interest factor alone will bring her many, many sales.'

Was there anything this extraordinary Scottish lady couldn't do?

THE LEGEND OF
SUSAN BOYLE

By late September, Susan's reputation as a star in her own right had been sealed. Early criticism that she only ever sang two songs had been drowned out by the medley of tunes she'd performed in the past couple of months — the critics didn't seem to realize that she was obliged to sing only those two songs, because she was on the *Britain's Got Talent* tour, rather than a tour of her own. There was also no slowdown in the number of stars stepping up to the plate to profess their admiration for her. Jon Bon Jovi became the latest — and perhaps most unlikely — star to express a desire to work with her.

Piers Morgan also spoke out about Susan again. It seemed that he, too, had benefitted from his association with her. Unlike Amanda, he was already making a name for himself in the States before Susan came along, but he believed she'd transformed his image.

'What propelled me to worldwide fame is largely Susan Boyle,' he said in the run-up to the release of Susan's first album. 'I have been passionate about my duty of care towards her, and I think that has changed attitudes towards me. But I feel adamant that the maelstrom resulting from this year's *BGT* finale was hugely overplayed. Susan Boyle will especially become the standard-bearer for the response to the criticism of Simon Cowell and the way he does his business. She's not some weirdo. Most people in showbusiness are a bit eccentric if you think about it. It doesn't mean they're not great talents. When people hear her album, they are going to see that she is phenomenal.'

Susan returned home from America for a well-deserved rest, and shortly afterwards plans for her to appear on *The X Factor* were announced. There was a brief health scare, when she was rushed to hospital with flu-like symptoms, but her health was bearing up well on the whole.

Susan was increasingly excited as the launch of the album neared. On her website, she called the album 'autobiographical', explaining, 'Some of the songs I chose because they had been favourites that I have sung for many years. One of the songs, I suppose you would call it a signature tune, "Wild Horses", has had a great reception and was first played on the radio by Terry Wogan. I have his autobiography at home and it seems very strange that he is now playing my record.'

Her grasp of modern technology continued apace: as well as her own website, on which she posted regular updates about how she was getting on, she also had a Facebook site, which had attracted 1.8 million fans. Although this doesn't quite rival the site for Michael Jackson, which has over 10 million members, it's still one of the largest sites on Facebook. Madonna has only managed 1.2 million, and that's considered an extremely reputable tally, while Whitney Houston has only 214,000.

Michael Bublé became Susan's newest celebrity admirer. 'I didn't understand Susan Boyle,' he said. 'I was cynical and critical because I had never seen her in that first show where she'd come up and says, "I want to be a singer," and the audience looks at her and says, "Oh please!" I got goosebumps. I'm going to go, when this record comes out, and buy twenty copies, because what a beautiful story of an underdog. It gives me faith in the human condition that we still have that kind of feeling that we actually want the good guy to win. It killed me. It really is a beautiful, beautiful story.'

And so the launch came about, as detailed in the first chapter of this book. Susan had done it, and she got the kind of reviews all entertainers crave:

'More restrained and emotionally resonant than seemed likely, and Boyle emerges with real dignity and class. Given the fleeting nature of her particular kind of fame, it may be her only mega-selling album: if so, she can be proud of it.'

new.uk.music.yahoo.com

'She's done well, has Susan Boyle, but whether she's got the talent and nerve to see her career through to the next stage is something only time will tell. In the meantime, this is a no-brainer for your gran's Christmas stocking.'

Lauren Murphy, entertainment.ie

'In "I Dreamed a Dream", from *Les Miserables,* her quieter singing, notable for its freshness and clarity of diction, evokes the spirit of a young woman without recourse to dramatics. Another winner is her gentle take on the Skeeter Davis song "The End Of The World".'

bbc.co.uk/music

'Boyle's voice is restrained, the orchestration is rich and the song choices demonstrate her vocal clarity and range . . . In our era of Auto-Tune and artificial glamour Boyle is a reminder of pure talent.'

virginmedia.com

Of course, the reviews couldn't resist mentioning the possibility of transient fame, but that didn't take into account one very important aspect of Susan's renown — she had cracked America. The only other British reality TV star to have made an impression in the US was Leona Lewis, and few British stars of any description had managed to achieve success Stateside. It was this fact, more than anything else, that suggested Susan would enjoy longevity in the music business, for there was no sign at all that the United States was tiring of its new heroine. Even back in Britain, as everyone conceded, there had never been a phenomenon like this.

The singer Seal, another Boyle admirer, thought much the same. 'It's good entertainment, but I question sometimes whether it's the best thing for our industry,' he said of reality television talent shows. 'Susan Boyle is an exception. I seriously believe that Susan couldn't give a stuff about being famous. She sings because it's in her — she's a true artist. She sings because it's her form of expression and if she doesn't she will become ill. It's her way of release.' High praise indeed.

There had been reports of Susan suffering from bad attacks of nerves, but those close to her were adamant that she was learning to cope. 'She is adjusting very well to the circumstances of her fame,' said Susan's voice coach Fred O'Neil. 'I don't remember her ever being a nervous performer, but I think that it's a different set of circumstances and she will cope given time. I feel that she's very happy in her life, so I'm sure that will come through. She comes and goes whenever she likes at home [in Blackburn] with no problems. She has time to live a normal life and the stresses are off her. She sounds very happy with life.'

Susan was merely getting used to a new and extraordinary set of circumstances and there was bound to be a period of adjustment when she would have to learn to pace herself.

In London, there was a great hoo-ha when Simon Cowell celebrated his fiftieth birthday with a huge party. Le tout showbiz was there — with one exception. Apparently the £2 million bash held in a Palladian mansion called Wrotham Park, with a guest list that included Cheryl Cole, Dannii Minogue, Kate Moss, the *Britain's Got Talent* judges and others too numerous to mention, was a slightly raunchy affair and Susan would have been out of place. And although she was probably more famous than anyone else there, Susan had not yet begun to take part in the schmooze fest of awards ceremonies and showbusiness parties that accompany life in the music business.

In the wake of her album release, her brother Gerry explained it: 'Susan is doing really well just now and is just resting up after visiting America,' he said. 'She didn't go to Simon Cowell's fiftieth birthday party because she didn't want a lot of attention on her, but she is delighted with her new CD.'

Indeed, Gerry was very keen to talk about the CD. It had been thrilling for the Boyles to watch Susan blossom over the past few months. They had all had their various concerns about her, especially in the wake of their mother's death, and they were delighted that she was suddenly having such an interesting life. They, of course, had heard her singing from childhood and knew that this was a culmination of a dream Susan had nurtured for nearly fifty years.

'Both Susan's and my own personal favourite track is "I Dreamed A Dream" — I know it is corny but that is the song that really introduced her to the world and I think it is really well suited to her voice,' Gerry said. ' "Cry Me A River" is another strong song on the album, and she originally recorded it at Heartbeat Studios in Scotland many years ago. "Wild Horses", which she débuted on American television, is another good choice, as the classic Rolling Stones song shows off her vocal range. I think a lot of people will also love "Silent Night" because it is perfect for Christmas time and the holidays. Susan's version of "Daydream Believer" is a lot of fun and her version of "Up To The Mountain" is very rousing too. Overall the album is very well produced, but it still gives her the chance to showcase her vocals on tracks like "Amazing Grace", "How Great Thou Art" and "You'll See". I think that the song choice is very good and we are all crossing our fingers that her fans will like it and it will be a hit too.' Needless to say, it was.

There was more admiration from yet another unlikely quarter, the rapper 50 Cent. 'Susan Boyle is hot right now,' he said. 'I got to get her on a track, for real. We'd make a hit. Everyone is talking about her, the lady from *Britain's Got Talent*. She's got an amazing voice, and together we'd get everyone dancing. I'm always looking to do something new and she's cool, so I'll ask somebody to let her know. I'd love to take her clubbing, show her around my world. She'd have a great time.' Was he joking? Who knew?

The *Britain's Got Talent* judges had certainly been vindicated about their choice. Amanda was delighted with the way the record was selling, but given that she'd seen the reaction to Susan from day one, she had suspected this might be on the cards.

'It's incredible, but to be honest I'm not at all surprised,' she told *Hello!* magazine. 'She's phenomenal, and her story has gone worldwide, so of course her album sales would do the same.' As for the earlier teething problems, Amanda felt the same way as the other judges: 'You've got to remember her audition,' she explained. 'She was feisty and strong, and funny and flirty — she's a really big character. She's had to deal with a lot in her life, she got through it and she's a stronger person for it, so we mustn't underestimate her strengths. I think we will have a chance to catch up with her before Christmas. She's been all over the world and none of us have been able to pin her down!'

Susan was also on the verge of becoming a wealthy woman. No one knew how much she was earning from it all, but there were estimates of over £5 million. Whatever the truth of it, Susan was finally going to get the peace of mind she craved. Despite all the comments about her single status, she appeared to be more interested in preparing for the future than finding love: 'Och, there's no time for that now!' she told one reporter. 'I'm far too busy! What a laugh. I dream about security, I dream about one day finding the right person. My advice to those who dare to dream is don't give up. If I can do it, anyone else can too.'

Simon Cowell was, of course, earning money out of Susan, but he was adamant that he would have walked away from it all had Susan not been able to cope. 'I said to [her family] at the time, the truth is, if this is too much for her or if she doesn't want to do it, we'll rip the contract up,' he said. 'No-one is going to be forced into doing anything. We were going to make a lot of money, and we have, but I would have walked away from that, I would.'

Simon had also been criticized for making more money out of Susan than she was, though that's not entirely fair, for like it or not, that is the way the music industry works. The artist is paid a percentage of record sales, thought in Susan's case to be about 15 per cent, because it's the record company that's taking the risk. Susan was certainly not being treated unfairly. Indeed, the money she was set to earn would have been life-changing in itself, even without her new career.

In the run-up to Christmas, Susan returned home, having decided that she would after all keep Blackburn as her base. As her global fame continued to spread and she travelled more and more, she needed a base where she felt entirely at home, near the friends and family who were helping her cope. Her newfound status continued to provoke changes: Susan was forced to beef up security at her home, although she continued to be as friendly as ever to fans and reporters. She willingly posed for photographs, signed autographs and waved cheerily to passers-by — there was no sign whatsoever of any diva-like behaviour. There was also no sign of a return of the tensions that beset her during the competition. Now she appeared to be taking it all in her stride.

Plans for the television special, *I Dreamed A Dream: The Susan Boyle Story,* were progressing, with yet another of Susan's dreams about to come true. This was kept from her until the last minute, but it had been arranged that she would finally sing a duet with her great idol, Elaine Paige. The two of them performed Elaine's hit 'I Know Him So Well', an experience that Susan clearly found overwhelming: 'I never thought I would see myself standing on the same stage with such an icon from West End theatre, let alone singing with her,' she said.

Elaine was as warm as ever: 'It was a pleasure to finally sing with Susan; she was a delight to work with and I think we did more than justice to one of my favourite songs,' she said.

The duet went down a treat in the United States. One of the many fan sites that had been set up in the wake of the audition was www.susan-boyle.co.uk, and a typical posting from a US fan was as follows: 'Everyone here is *so* excited and thrilled about Susan's duet with Elaine and wanting more!' said Misti in Seattle. 'In fact we are very happy for Elaine as most of us had not even heard of her before and now she is also going to have a wonderful career here in the USA, as well as her British one. She was so sweet to Susan at the beginning when others were making fun of her and she has been so gracious about being the "guest" and giving Susan her "star" time. They both just sparkle together and sound wonderful. I am so hoping they do an album together and bet they will as the producers will not let *this* money maker slide through their hands.'

Would Susan be responsible for giving Elaine Paige's career a boost in the United States? What a turnaround that would be.

Susan couldn't resist having a little fun while filming the show. She also performed 'Who I Was Born To Be', but alarmed production staff when she did a little dance during a piano solo, possibly as a way of releasing the tension she was feeling. The programme was, naturally, presented by Piers Morgan, and there was a highly emotional moment when he presented her with a gold disc and Susan broke down in tears. 'It feels bloody fantastic,' she said. 'I think my mum would be proud. She was quite a lady, y'know.'

The programme attracted over 10 million viewers when it was aired — twice the number that had tuned in the previous evening to see Cheryl Cole's *Night In*.

Susan retained her hold on the top of the album charts on both sides of the Atlantic and explained to Piers how she drew strength from her religious faith: 'On a personal level, church is very important to me; it's the central part of my faith and I recognize that God gives you gifts that you have to use to the best of your ability,' she said. She was therefore doubly delighted when, on a promotional visit to France, she was surrounded by a gaggle of fans who just happened to be Parisian nuns. It seemed the French loved her as much as everyone else, and she caused a sensation whenever she appeared on French talk shows. The same was also true in Germany, where she performed in *Das Supertalent* in Cologne. Her appeal was truly global and her story seemed to resonate with people all over the world.

Despite all this success, Susan remained as modest as ever. In an interview with *People* magazine, she claimed that her life had hardly changed: 'I still have my former life,' she said. 'I still live in the same house.

My life hasn't changed. I travel more. I see places I never thought I would see. There is nothing I miss, because I have everything I had before — it's just a little more interesting now. I met Donny Osmond. He was very nice. We talked about how important it was to stay grounded. He bought me some purple roses, and they were very beautiful.' As for the most important individual in the proceedings . . . 'Pebbles is blissfully unaware of everything that is going on,' said Susan — the little cat must have been the only individual in Susan's life who was. 'She lives with a very lovely lady while I am away working, and she is thriving. I visit her when I can, and I can travel knowing that she is in safe hands and being pampered.'

It wasn't easy nowadays for Susan to go anywhere unnoticed. On her return to Scotland, she turned up unannounced at Princes Mall in Edinburgh and caused a sensation, singing part of 'Wild Horses' and signing autographs.

Meanwhile, Susan's gold dust continued to work its magic. No one could claim she had brought fame and fortune to Simon Cowell, who had been at the top of the celebrity tree for some time, but she certainly hadn't done him any harm. It emerged in December that Cowell was set to become the first-ever reality television billionaire, and though that can't be attributed specifically to Susan, she had helped him on his way.

No one was surprised when Susan's 'I Dreamed A Dream' audition turned out to be the most watched clip of the year on YouTube, with 120 million hits on that site alone. Was there no end to Susan's success? But there was a serious side to it all, too. Susan had done it all for her mother, Bridget, but Bridget was no longer there to see her famous, talented daughter, the one she'd fretted over for so many years. 'She's not alive to see how proud I could have made her,' said Susan sadly to one interviewer — it was the one rather poignant note at a time of great triumph.

Susan was having to learn to pace herself, though. A publicity trip to Canada that was supposed to have taken place in November was postponed to December and then postponed again due to renewed fears about her health. In fact, all Susan needed was another rest, and her fans seemed to know and understand this. A typical posting on Susan's official website from someone called Shirleyio said, 'Susan's management team has had her hopping back and forth across the Atlantic three times in a short period of time. That much travel is excruciating. She wants to spend time with her family at Christmas. When she needs a break, she should take it. Her team knows that.'

Susan was also taking care of her voice. She was working with another voice coach, Yvie Burnett, who taught her that if her career was to be a long-term one, it was essential that she get the training in. It wasn't just a case of dealing with physical exhaustion; Susan had to treat her voice like an instrument. She was beginning to learn what was good for it and how long it would have to rest.

Meanwhile, people started to make a fortune out of Susan Boyle—related memorabilia on eBay, a great deal of which was unauthorized.

It was 'despicable profiteering making unscrupulous people millions of pounds', said Max Clifford, a spokesperson for Simon Cowell. 'Susan has had a wonderful year and I know she'll be upset about some of this stuff, especially as it may be fooling fans into thinking it has something to do with her. It's a sad fact of life that there are always people who don't care how low they sink to profit from others, and some of this is really cheap and nasty. I can assure you that Simon Cowell's lawyers are taking a very close look at every single item using Susan.'

One person who was hoping to benefit was school janitor Thomas Crawford, who had a copy of the Whitburn Community Council charity CD, which had been made ten years earlier and included a track featuring Susan singing. As a bona fide piece of memorabilia, he was entitled to sell it.

'I played the drums with a band playing one of the tracks on the CD and my dad kept it,' he related. 'When we heard that someone got $2,000 in America for one of the CDs, we decided to put it up for sale on eBay and see what happens and we'll share the money. The bidding starts at £500 and the buy-it-now price is £2,500. Our band, The Fines, used to play at many of the venues Susan used to sing in and she's a lovely lady.'

On this occasion the merchandise was totally above board, but fake memorabilia was something else. 'She's very upset about it all,' said a friend of the family who didn't wish to be named. 'Susan has always been in this for the singing, not the money, but now people are jumping on the bandwagon to make cash for themselves. It's sickening really. Susan's done a lot for charity, and the only thing she's endorsed is the eBay sale of a singing trophy she won last year at Blackburn Bowling Club. The money is going to raise cash for the CHAS appeal, which is close to Susan's heart. The bidding starts this weekend. There's nothing else she endorses on eBay, and I hope people don't waste their money on any of it.'

Susan certainly wasn't motivated by the money herself. Having been brought up in modest circumstances, she'd retained modest tastes, and wasn't planning on a big splurge any time soon. 'I will probably be able to buy the house I live in, which was my family home, which is fantastic. I don't have any other big ambitions really. I have bought some new furniture. You've got to keep your house looking nice, haven't you? I would like to do something good with the money — be useful to other people, help them. I have a few ideas in mind.' The new furniture turned out to be a sofa and a fridge. Is it any wonder she was universally adored?

Talk of a film about Susan's life continued, with more actresses being suggested to portray her. Catherine Zeta-Jones was certainly the most glamorous option, but Susan's brother Gerry was more pragmatic. 'There have been scripts made from a lot less than Susan's story, which by any standards is remarkable,' he said. 'I would not be surprised in the least if there was a film made of her life and I would personally like to see Kathy Bates play my sister. Other British actresses like Brenda Blethyn would also be great and I just hope they get Brad Pitt to play me! Susan is planning to be with her family over Christmas and New Year and it will be great to have her home with us over the holidays. If an unknown woman from a small town in Scotland can go on to become the biggest-selling artist in America then anything is possible. We are all very proud of Susan and her dream really has come true with these fantastic CD sales. I've seen a tremendous change in my sister over the last year and she really has a strong team of people surrounding her now. I think that the sales of her CD will also be strong in other markets around the world because Susan's story is so unique and it gives a lot of people hope.'

Gerry was being called in to act as his sister's representative and spokesman from time to time. In December Susan won the Top Scot award at the Glenfiddich Spirit of Scotland awards, but it was Gerry who collected the prize on her behalf. 'It's amazing that she's won this,' he said. 'She still thinks she's the little lady from Blackburn. It's a tremendous achievement in what has been a tremendous year and she is delighted and thrilled.'

Scot of the year! Susan's story got more extraordinary by the day, but what was particularly heartening was the happy note on which she ended the year. Despite all the dire warnings about the dangers of putting a vulnerable woman in the media spotlight, Susan had gone from strength to strength. She had found the right balance in her life. The family home in Blackburn provided the safe haven, while visiting the rest of the world allowed her to spread her wings and fly. Her stamina was impressive, too: there might have been the odd postponement, such as the Canadian tour, but she still managed to pack a huge amount into her life, particularly now that she had proper back-up and moral support.

Her brothers Gerry and John gave an interview to *Hello!* magazine, in which they talked at length about their pride at what Susan had done. 'They'd sold out in my local store, but as I stood there looking at the empty CD case, sitting alongside the albums of all those established worldwide stars, I felt like I could burst with pride,' said John. 'There she was, my baby sister! Her dream had come true and, like the rest of the family, I couldn't have been more delighted for her. Susan is fine. I gave her a wee ring earlier, because obviously I do worry about her — she'll always be my baby sister.'

'But we've told Susan that if she ever feels like it's getting too much for her, she only has to say,' added John. 'As a family, we'd spot the signs and know when to step in, but sometimes all she needs is a call from one of us.'

As for Simon Cowell, Gerry said, 'The man's a legend and has been so supportive. He's always seemed very sincere and genuinely concerned for Susan's wellbeing and happiness. I think she's very lucky to have come to his attention.'

As the year drew to an end, the scale of Susan's achievements became even clearer. *I Dreamed A Dream* was in its third week at number one in the United States, Canada, the UK, Ireland, Australia, New Zealand, Japan and Switzerland. It had received RIAA Triple Platinum Certification, meaning that over three million copies had been shipped to retailers in the US. It was the biggest-selling album of 2009, the first album released that year to hold the number one slot for three consecutive weeks and the highest-selling album ever for a début artist.

Worldwide, over seven million copies had been shipped and Susan had become the fastest selling global female début artist ever. All told, it had been quite a year.

Susan Boyle had done the unthinkable. She hadn't only changed the face of reality TV; she had changed the face of showbusiness. She had become an inspiration and a heroine to millions across the globe and become more famous than many long-established showbusiness stars. She had given the lie to the notion that you had to be young and nubile to succeed and, most powerfully of all, she was living proof that you should never give up on your dream. Everything about Susan was likeable. Her straightforward demeanour, her childishly innocent answers to questions and her utterly unspoilt behaviour had set her apart from the divas of this world and made her an icon for our times.

But why? And how? Just what was it that set Susan apart from the scores of other showbusiness wannabes, plenty of whom had genuine talents of their own? Why did this shy little woman from the backwaters of Scotland turn overnight into one of the most famous people in the world? For Susan had become more than an icon, more than a global phenomenon. Something about her reached into the spirit of the listener or the viewer and spoke to something deep in their hearts. But what was it? And how had it come about?

A Very Modern
Fairytale

There is no doubting the fact that Susan Boyle is a phenomenon. In the film *42nd Street,* one of the most famous instructions ever delivered to a performer is given: 'And Sawyer, you're going out a youngster, but you've got to come back a star.' Susan certainly wasn't a youngster, as the expressions of shock on the faces of the audience at her first audition testified when she confessed to reaching the ripe old age of forty-seven, but in every other way, that was Susan's story. She went out a Scottish spinster and came back a global superstar.

The effect, as has been described elsewhere in this book, was immediate. The Susan Boyle sensation did not take months to build, nor was it an orchestrated campaign: overnight, the world fell in love. It wasn't romantic, passionate love, but the love of self-recognition, mixed with admiration for bravery, stoicism, endurance and grace. We all have dreams we've never realized, and most of us don't have the guts to fulfil them either. Susan, who had endured so much in her early life, and more recently at the hands of the press, turned out to have a great deal more courage than many people who would consider themselves stronger than her. It was this that gave her such global appeal and spoke to her many fans throughout the world.

And so inevitably the analysis of Susan's appeal began. The United States had been particularly swept away by Susan, and a whole host of posts appeared on the influential American website The Huffington Post. Pop critic Mark Blankenship cited two reasons why Susan had captivated the world: 'She rebukes the bitchy cynicism that often defines reality talent shows,' was the first, followed by, 'Susan Boyle isn't young. The Susan Boyle Story is even more powerful because Boyle isn't a geeky teenager,' he continued. 'You can look at the most maladjusted adolescent and think, "Well, she'll grow out of it. There's still hope." But when a woman is an outsider at forty-seven, it's easy to think it's too late and that she's doomed to a permanent life on the fringes . . . Watching an older person — especially an older person who doesn't seem very hip — prove she still has time to emerge from her cocoon is exciting because it reminds us that we can still sort through our own problems.'

Michael Russnow, a professional television screenwriter, wrote about the audience's perception of Susan as a bit of an oddball who they were preparing to mock. 'All this foreshadowed the commencement of her singing, which instantaneously evaporated the misperceptions we'd invented, causing most of us to respond with unmitigated shock — including the judges, assuming they, too, were in the dark — morphing instantaneously into collective joy,' he wrote. 'Joy' was certainly one of the sentiments that Susan aroused: the spectacle of the underdog quite stupendously breaking through.

Letty Cottin Pogrebin, founding editor of *Ms.* magazine, identified three elements that made Susan's story stand out. 'Partly, I think it's the age thing, the fact that a woman closing in on fifty had the courage to compete with the kids — and blew them out of the water,' she wrote. 'Then, too, we were weeping for the years of wasted talent, the career that wasn't, the time lost — both for Susan Boyle and two generations of her putative fans. But I'd wager that most of our joyful tears were fueled by the moral implicit in Susan's fairy-tale performance: "You can't tell a book by its cover". For such extraordinary artistry to emerge from a woman that plain-spoken, unglamorous, and unyoung was an intoxicating reminder of the wisdom in that corny old cliché.'

There were many more Susan-related blogs on the site: she had become an object of absolute fascination, with a story that would bear dissecting over and over again.

It was certainly the case that Susan had roundly disabused the prevalent notion in modern day life that success is entirely dependent on youth and looks.

'Only the pretty are expected to achieve,' wrote Colette Douglas Home. 'Not only do you have to be physically appealing to deserve fame; it seems you now have to be good-looking to merit everyday common respect. If, like Susan (and like millions more), you are plump, middle-aged and too poor or too unworldly to follow fashion or have a good hairdresser, you are a non-person.' Except that she wasn't. She was a global phenomenon.

Although Susan herself continues to be as bemused as anyone by what has happened to her, she has not spent a great deal of time analysing it all. She, too, felt that she simply resonated with the global audience because of the world's tendency to judge people on how they look. 'Modern society is too quick to judge people on their appearances,' she has said. 'There is not much you can do about it; it is the way they think; it is the way they are. But maybe this could teach them a lesson, or set an example.' And when she did decide to smarten up, she didn't go over the top — Susan is still definitely Susan.

To Lisa Schwarzbaum, writing on Pop-Watch, Susan was something more: a direct appeal to the spiritual in every one of us. 'In our pop-minded culture so slavishly obsessed with packaging — the right face, the right clothes, the right attitudes, the right Facebook posts — the unpackaged artistic power of the unstyled, un-hip, un-kissed Ms. Boyle let me feel, for the duration of one blazing showstopping ballad, the meaning of human grace,' she wrote. 'She pierced my defenses. She reordered the measure of beauty. And I had no idea until tears sprang how desperately I need that corrective from time to time.'

And then there was the issue of self-belief. Susan had displayed that, too, encouraged by the mother she loved and missed so much, and that was also to be applauded.

'In a world sometimes rife with bloated résumés, stage mothers, fawning friends, self-adulation, narcissism and bedroom shelves holding too many meaningless trophies from middle school, here is a woman who took an accurate measure of her worth and put it to the test in the white-hot crucible of reality TV,' wrote Jeanne McManus in the *Washington Post*. Nor is it exaggerating to say that Susan's tale is also about the redemptive power of love: in this case the love between a mother and daughter. Bridget loved Susan and therefore encouraged her to make something of herself; Susan loved Bridget and so took her life — or at least her dignity — in her hands by going out on that stage in Glasgow to audition.

Feminists, of course, were all over the story, with all it had to say about the nature of shallow appearances as opposed to fundamental true worth. But Susan wasn't the first not obviously beautiful singer to make an impact, a point made by R. M. Campbell, a Seattle-based music critic, for the site The Gathering Note. 'There's no shortage of first-class voices out there, but Boyle has a unique story: she's unattractive,' she wrote, a little harshly perhaps. 'She's a bit like Ella Fitzgerald. Fitzgerald was overweight and wore glasses — everything a woman entertainer shouldn't be. It's really, really hard to make a career if a woman isn't attractive. But Fitzgerald was a great singer and a great musician, and she rose above her physical circumstances. Her career lasted sixty years.'

It was probably a little late for Susan to clock up a comparable length music career, but even so, it was a notable comparison to one of the singing greats.

Susan's story was also a comforting, and rare, example of the good guys coming first. In life, and especially in showbusiness, it tends to be the ruthless, the ones prepared to play hardball, who win through. Gentle, modest and self-effacing are not qualities often attributed to the most successful people in this world. This time, however, it was different.

'People like Susan Boyle are the glue of our society and it's nice when finally something good happens to them,' wrote the *Star-Ledger* of New Jersey. 'It is an honour to watch a middle-aged, rounded woman with little or no make-up and an old dress go up on stage and beat ridicule with an amazing voice. A story even Hans Christian Andersen couldn't make up.'

The *Daily News* of New York was also keen to sum up Susan's triumphant moment.

'The audience was laughing at the notion that this totally undistinguished person would presume to dream that she could enter pop stardom, one of the most glamorous kingdoms in the world,' it said. 'Then when she soared, that all went away, and because she overcame this unspoken assumption that she was insignificant, she shone far more brightly than some polished and glamorous young performer from whom we would have expected a moment of brilliance.' Again, it was a case of not judging a book by its cover.

It wasn't unusual for journalists and bloggers to tackle the big issues of the day — something Susan had certainly become. What was a little more unusual was when the academic community started to take an interest, too. Susan's story had become so important, so universal and so personal to viewers from all over the world that Dr Robert Canfield, professor of anthropology at Washington University in St Louis, wrote a treatise about the phenomenon entitled 'Susan Boyle and the Power of the Moral Imagination'. In it he pointed out that the lyrics of the song Susan chose to sing at her audition were actually about hopes dashed, a life wasted, the promise of youth thrown away. What song could have been more suitable for Susan to sing? Patronized, ignored and bullied as a child, what dreams had Susan dreamt that had come to ashes and ended in nought? And yet there was this late flowering hope, the realization that her life might amount to something after all.

'Buried within the human psyche are feelings, yearnings, anxieties too deep for words, usually,' he wrote. 'Always it is something outside ourselves that touches us, somehow, where we feel most deeply. At such moments we remember that we are humans — not merely creatures, but human beings, profoundly and deeply shaped by a moral sensibility so powerful that it breaks through our inhibitors; it can burst out, explode into public view, to our own astonishment. And sometimes that objective form — a person, an event, an object, a song — embodies deeply felt sensibilities for a lot of us at once, so that we discover how much we share in our private worlds, worlds otherwise inaccessible to anyone else. It becomes a social event, so we can all rejoice, and weep, together.'

Susan had become such a phenomenon that she was almost instantly embraced by popular culture, too. There were instances of it happening in the UK, but again it was the United States that led the way, incorporating her into the artistic output of the pop culture it produced. *South Park* was the first off the mark, although it adhered to its usual vulgarity when Susan got a name check. Cartman goes off to round up his fellow South Park children to run away to join the pirates in Somalia, and Kyle leaves a letter to his parents, saying, 'Dear Mommy and Daddy — I am running away. Everyone at school is a f****** idiot and if one more person talks to me about that Susan Boyle performance of *Les Miserables* I was going to puke my b**** out through my mouth.' It was a compliment — of sorts.

After that, the references came thick and fast. *Late Night With Jimmy Fallon* had a comedy sketch that talked about the feel-good nature of the clip. It showed a series of office arguments, starting with a row over a lost document, continuing with one when the coffee machine breaks down and ended up with zombies breaking into the building. Every incidence pales into insignificance as each staff member is won over by the shot of Susan singing in her audition. 'That was amazing! I love that lady,' cried Jimmy Fallon at the end: he was not alone.

Next up it was the turn of America's most dysfunctional family, *The Simpsons*. It was the show's twentieth anniversary, and to mark the milestone there was a show called *Springfield's Got Talent.* Homer Simpson took to the stage, introducing himself: 'My name is Homer Simpson, I'm thirty-nine years old and, well, I've never been kissed,' he began. 'My dream is to be a great singer like Susan Boyle.'

In May, a new video game, *The Sims 3,* came out, featuring a character based on Susan. Then in June, Britain finally got in on the act when a Radio 4 short story entitled *I Dreamed A Dream* was broadcast, drawing comparisons between Susan and the Scottish prime minister, Gordon Brown — a recurrent subject for cartoonists at the time. In November, it was back to the United States and the series *30 Rock,* in which the character Kathy Geiss, played by Marceline Hugot, sang in Susan's style while a row raged on in front of her.

When you Google the name Susan Boyle, over 18 million hits come up (and that's at the time of writing — it's increasing all the time). The audition clip continues to be one of the most widely viewed on the web, not least because, as well as gaining new fans, established ones tend to watch it time and again.

At the centre of this maelstrom, Susan carries on her life, still bewildered by the reaction she's provoked, but accepting her glorious fate and enjoying the attention after spending so long in the shadows. She wants and loves her new life, and anyone who doubts her ability to deal with the limelight would do well to remember that.

What, ultimately, has made Susan so universally loved is that she is everywoman. Everyone in the world has a bit of Susan Boyle in them — the frightened wee girl treated badly at school and dismissed as an adult — but Susan proved that these are handicaps that can be overcome. Everyone has dreamed a dream of some description, though few of us are able to follow it through. After all, it takes guts to leave the safety zone and expose yourself to the eyes of an unforgiving world — something Susan did and has kept on doing. Ultimately, the Susan Boyle story is about hope.

The following comments are taken from the numerous fan sites for Susan that have sprung up on the web.

She's gorgeousssssssssss! I love reading articles where the writers are trying to guess why she's become such a huge sensation. They're always looking for an answer that sounds so complicated when it's so easy to see. As soon as she started to sing, her voice owned the stage and everyone listening.

It became obvious that interest in her was remaining very international. When I heard fans of other (much younger) singers bragging about how they'd come out in front, I'd think, 'just you wait — your singer does not have the international audience Susan has won already!'

Most singers never achieve this kind of world wide recognition, Susan did it with one brilliant performance, and has followed that up with one brilliant album. And just think — there's more to come!

What an amazing interview [on Australian radio] — Susan sounds so happy and grounded — she is truly accepting her remarkable gift of music and is coming to believe in herself and her abilities — what a thrill it is to watch the transformation of a human being into knowing and living 'Who I Was Born To Be'.

12/15/09 — Updated information on
Susan's YouTube Hits

Greetings!!
    Hello to you out there in Susanland. What

a ride it has been trying to collect the new videos of Susan for News, tributes, interviews and her performances across the globe! WOW!!

Thank you all for being patient while this update information has taken me a little over a month to get, it was so well worth it! Also I have combined Susan's Wild Horses song only (not just viewing on AGT) to "Other Songs Sung". This does NOT cut away to having lost hits, just combining them.

So here are the results to the best of my ability. First you will see results from last time and of course the results for this time.

Auditions — 194,721,285–203,397,586

Semi-finals & Results — 61,568,444–66,271,003

Finals & Results — 19,934,616–21,354,863

Interviews & News Headlines — 26,819,361–44,144,917

BGT Tour — 1,400,205–1,816,409

Other Songs Sung — 33,137,701–42,077,564

Tributes — 656,087–4,624,972

Total — 340,808,132–383,687,314

Difference of — 42,879,182

All this from Sept. 9th to Dec. 15th!! There

is just NO STOPPING our LADY is there!?
Have a Merry Christmas!!

Wow!!!
She is stunningly gorgeous in this . . . so happy and so beautifully made-up with a truly becoming hair style!

THANX for posting these SUE-PER pictures — any one know exactly when Susan performed — is it another NEW dress??? . . . a delicious plum color, a bit less dress, and a bit more skin, obvious hanging earrings, and a very soft hair do, much like that in Paris . . . any dates and what she sang??????

Susan will soon have a house full of plaques and awards. I wonder if Pebbles will get an award as well?

Susan Boyle is a brilliant vocalist . . . she has attained her 'dream' and we should all salute her talent . . . her voice brings a shiver up the spine and a tear to the eye. Thank you Susan for sharing!!!

My brother just sent this to me today and I was blown away. She is great!!! What a way for an underdog to set the whole world on its ear. She is a true treasure. A true talent that can finally be shared with both the world and her very lucky cat. God bless her.

i've run into a handful of ppl — and i do mean a handful; could count em on one hand — who are having a cow about the media 'hype' as they call it. It's not the media that has got the world on its ear. First it was her talent. Her stage presence and now her FANS. To say hype is to call us hype. *BGT* auditioned her but the world discovered her very much on its own. That's not hype. HYPE is britney spears doing all kinds of stupid stuff, getting in trouble with the law and doing smutty stuff deliberately just to get attention. That's media driven hype. This is NOT Susan!!!!

Susan is such an inspiration to people. I know, I suffer from clinical depression and when I hear her sing, she lifts my spirit. I would ask her 'What took you so long?' I wish her the best in everything she does. Don't ever stop singing.

Ever since I first saw Susan on *BGT* I've been a dedicated fan!
Susan is unique! Her wonderful voice and naturalness have gained her millions of fans worldwide!

Will never forget her first rendition of 'I Dreamed A Dream'! I have listened to that over and over again and still do after all these months. Like Barb, think I must be responsible for a few hundred 'hits' at least! LOL!

I just paid my daily visit to the YouTube Audition video as I promised. The dang thing always has me in tears. It's so incredible. Each viewing is as good as the first time seeing her. It's just so lovely.

A mega talent with a touching and beautiful story. Never gets old. Never.

Like Christine, I listen to this audition all the time. Even with her CD out I still watch it a lot. Somehow seeing the facial expressions and the dropped jaws make her story so potent. Her voice is heavenly and her CD gives us that but I must say that the YouTube gives us her story AND the angelic voice together. It is so sweet! I adore the CD too because I can take it with me to use in the car.

I would be delighted to play a part in bringing her up to #9 then 8, then 7 etc. I do not grow tired of this sublime and brilliant moment in contemporary music history. I just did it now and I will visit her audition YouTube daily or more if I have time.

Thank you Susan for all you've given us!

Magic — just pure magic!

I have listened to this first audition so many times and I never tire of it! It is incredible, and every time I watch it I am filled with the excitement and get the chills I had the very first time. The audience went mad and it was a most joyous experience.

The power in her voice and her interpretation of the song is without precedent. No wonder she got a standing ovation!

GO SUSAN GO!! WE LOVE YOU!

I have a most important message for Susan. My son-in-law has Alzheimer's and he has declared Susan as God's Christmas gift to us this year. The CD is played for him day and night and it always goes in the car with us. What a blessing she has been for our family and Joe . . . we'll soon have to buy a new copy . . . we're all looking forward to her next album. God bless you Susan.

Ignore those silly people who use archaic words to describe a phenomenon. Nasty comments, of course, should be challenged, but Susan has risen so far above most of those writing about her that their use of language is irrelevant. Just think — 2 trips to LA, one to New York, *X Factor* at home, Paris, Germany, own show on TV, duet with one of UKs most admired singers — WOW WOW WHAT A FEW WEEKS FOR A LOVELY LADY. Add to that TOP of the charts for 3 weeks all over the world. Yes, I think we can accept that our Susan has made it. Many of us have worried, prayed and hoped that she would succeed and our prayers have been answered a thousandfold. Well done, Susan, and well done, fans. Between us we have beaten the sneering blighters.

For the life of me, I can't figure out WHY they keep referring to her as 'mentally slow' — if she is considered as such, then I must be waaaay off the lower end of the scale!!

All the remarks I have ever heard Susan make during her interviews have been quick and clever! Combined with her great sense of humour, she is unique!

From the amazing show of affection and appreciation of world audiences and the amount of records she is breaking 'public opinion' feels the same way.

It doesn't surprise me that Susan would do

so well. Susan Boyle is a genuine person, not a made up Hollywood piece of cosmetic trash who can't sing marketed by the low lifes that compose the Hollywood elite. I live in LA and Susan from England is a wonderful breath of fresh air. She represents us; the real people. She is like the tea party patriots; the real people.

Even though I'm a Yank in the U.S. (of solid Irish background . . .), I am hoping that adding my meager 'tuppence' here will be acceptable; good! I was fifty-ten on Friday, April 10. After hearing Susan Boyle's voice this week, and being incredibly fortunate to have seen a number of original Broadway musicals live while growing up in New York, her voice is, hands — and feet! — down, one of the best I have ever heard. Combine that with her innocence, her pluck, and the 'Simonish' judgment — be honest — all of us made about her before she sang, and, well, GOOD FOR HER!! (It's about damn time, eh?)

Hi there, my name is Paul and I come from the same village as susan, and I will admit it, I have seen her but never in my wildest dreams did I think she could sing!! until that is, 8.03 on Saturday night when I was completely blown away by the best singing voice I have heard since debbie harry. I was babysitting my little nephew zack at the time, and as her beautiful tonsils pelted out the classic song from my favourite musical, me and my younger nephew both knew something special was in the making! I actually love u, and would happily pay 8.99 for a susan boyle album!

Without doubt the most magical and moving thing i have ever seen on my tv in all my 45 years!!! I have probably seen it 40 times already and i still cry tears of joy every time!!

Susan you're the woman next door, the type of person nobody takes much notice of, for some reason when you get to your age and beyond we become nothing more than a ghost to millions, they do not see us! In my now dark days both your wonderful personality and beautiful voice made my heart sing again, thank you for being there for me on that night, with that song. I hope one day you will find a wonderful man who can look beyond vanity, I hope you are kissed for the first time. Never give up the dream, make it come true.

Excellent! What a voice! I've watched clip

over and over and it truly is beautiful. I believe YOUR dream is about to happen and you'll be up there with the stars VERY soon. Congratulations on making the first step to success (and I'm sure you've made the villagers of Blackburn and Scots everywhere immensely proud). Very best for the future girl, you certainly deserve it :o)

ABOUT THE AUTHOR

Alice Montgomery is a freelance author living and working in London.

We hope you have enjoyed this Large Print book. Other Thorndike, Wheeler, Kennebec, and Chivers Press Large Print books are available at your library or directly from the publishers.

For information about current and upcoming titles, please call or write, without obligation, to:

Publisher
Thorndike Press
295 Kennedy Memorial Drive
Waterville, ME 04901
Tel. (800) 223-1244

or visit our Web site at:

http://gale.cengage.com/thorndike

OR

Chivers Large Print
published by BBC Audiobooks Ltd
St James House, The Square
Lower Bristol Road
Bath BA2 3SB
England
Tel. +44(0) 800 136919
email: bbcaudiobooks@bbc.co.uk
www.bbcaudiobooks.co.uk

All our Large Print titles are designed for easy reading, and all our books are made to last.